AF003

MASSIMILIANO AFIERO

AXIS FORCES
3

WW2 AXIS
FORCES

The Axis Forces 003 - First edition July 2017 by Soldiershop.com.
Cover & Art Design by soldiershop factory. ISBN code: 978-88-93272650

In merito alla specifica serie Italia storia ebook serie Ritterkreuz l'editore Soldiershop informa che non essendone l'autore ne il primo editore del materiale pervenuto dall'associazione Ritterkreuz, declina ogni responsabilità in merito al suo contenuto di testi e/o immagini e la sua correttezza. A tal proposito segnaliamo che la pubblicazione Ritterkreuz tratta esclusivamente argomenti a carattere storico-militare e non intende esaltare alcun tipo di ideologia politica presente o del passato cosi come non intende esaltare alcun tipo di regime politico del secolo precedente ed alcuna forma di razzismo.

Note editoriali dell'edizione cartacea

The Axis Forces

in World War Two 1939-1945

The Axis Forces number 3 – July 2017

Direction and editing: Via San Giorgio, 11 – 80021 Afragola (NA) -ITALY

Managing and Chief Editor: Massimiliano Afiero

Email: maxafiero@libero.it

Website: www.maxafiero.it

Contributors

Stefano Canavassi, Carlos Caballero Jurado, Rene Chavez, Carlo Cucut, Dmitry Frolov, Eduardo M. Gil Martínez, Antonio Guerra, John B. Köser, Lars Larsen, Christophe Leguérandais, Peter Mooney, Erik Norling, Scott Revell, Raphael Riccio, Marc Rikmenspoel, Johannes Scharf, Charles Trang, Cesare Veronesi, Sergio Volpe

Editorial

With this third issue of the magazine we take another step forward with our publication, which we hope will continue to spread all over the world, both in digital format and in paper format, in the name of historical truth. Finally, we have begun to receive comments and advice on our magazine sent by our readers, all fortunately positive, but also suggestions on the editorial line to follow in the coming issues. Many readers have asked us to provide more coverage in the magazine to the formations of all the countries of the Axis, to keep faith with the title of the magazine, dealing in addition to the military units of Italy, Germany and Japan, also to units from Romania, Hungary, Finland And Slovakia, as well as of course foreign volunteer formations. Another suggestion is that in addition to addressing only ground units, aviation and Navy topics, which thus far have been excluded from discussion, should also be covered. Of course, we will take into account all of these suggestions, to meet the needs of our readers and we promise you that beginning with the next issue something new will be seen. In this third issue, I hope you will find interesting articles and topics, but as always, we invite you to send us further tips and suggestions to better meet your military history enthusiasts needs. A warm greeting to everyone and welcome to the next issue.

Massimiliano Afiero

Contents

Attack against the 'Stalin Line'
by Massimiliano Afiero

The 'Stalin Line' was a fortified line consisting of concrete bunkers, machine gun nests, tanks buried up to their turrets, mine fields and other defensive works of all types, with a depth of about eight kilometers. It had been built along the Soviet border with Latvia and Estonia.

March of the *Totenkopf* June-July 1941.

A *Totenkopf* soldier, 1941.

The fortifications of the "Stalin Line" were protected by miles of barbed wire and many minefields (NA).

It was a formidable but not totally insurmountable obstacle. This was due in part because the Soviets had not had enough time to complete all of the work and there were many "weak" points, on paper, that would be easy to break through. By order of Manstein, it was to be the *Totenkopf* itself that would smash through the Soviet defenses of the Stalin Line, a sacrificial mission.

On 6 July 1941, following a violent artillery bombardment, the *Totenkopf* troops went on the attack: moving from the Rosenov area, the SS troops attacked the positions at Sebesh. The enemy defenses in that area were very strong: thick coils of barbed wire, minefields, dug-in tanks transformed into fixed artillery positions, bunkers and anti-tank ditches.

Totenkopf engineers worked very hard to clear lanes through these positions (NA).

Totenkopf soldiers attacking the *"Stalin Line"* (NA).

SS troops moving to attack against an enemy position, July 1941.

These positions extended for six or seven kilometers in depth. Every individual bunker had to be attacked and taken with great determination. Grenadiers and assault engineers were able to make headway thanks to the support of mortars and flamethrowers. Each enemy position was cleaned out with hand grenades and machine pistol fire. Hand-to-hand fighting erupted everywhere. The troops of *SS-Tot.Inf.Rgt.3*, commanded by *SS-Staf.* Kleinheisterkamp, led the assault; *I.* and *II.Bataillon* ran up against several enemy positions that had not been touched by the *Stuka* attacks, and encountered stiff resistance. The *III./SS-Tot.Inf.Rgt.3*, commanded by *SS-Stubaf*. Otto Baum[1], led the other two battalions in the capture of a hill, supporting the attack with fire from its heavy weapons. The Soviet artillery continued to hit the attack front of the German units without letup, significantly slowing down the advance.

SS troops on the outskirts of a recently captured village in flames. **SS motorcycle scouts.**

SS troops attacking enemy positions, July 1941.

SS-Gruppenführer Eicke had gone up to the front line himself to observe the attack by his men, following the *9./SS-Tot.Inf.Rgt.3*. An enemy artillery shell fell quite close to the *Totenkopf* commander, causing killed and wounded, but miraculously leaving Eicke unharmed. Covered with dust, more furious than before, he yelled to his men: "*..continue to advance*".

Eicke in his *Kubelwagen* (*Bundesarchiv*).

A *Totenkopf Pak* on the outskirts of a village.

The leading German assault groups soon reached a concrete bunker with walls up to two meters thick; the assault engineers from Ullrich's battalion blew up several bunkers using explosive charges. At the same time, the SS engineers were also busy building makeshift bridges over the Velikaya River to allow the division's troops to cross. The advance to Opotschka now seemed possible, but the fighting was not yet over.

The attack against the second defensive line then began. By the end of the evening, the SS troops had established positions near Waselkowa. A bridge was thrown over the Welikaja River thanks to the efforts of *2.Kp./SS-Tot.Pi.-Btl.* led by *SS-Ostuf.* Monich[2]. The Soviets mounted fierce counterattacks throughout the night, attempting to reorganize their defenses. Around midnight, following a conference at von Manstein's headquarters, Theodor Eicke's vehicle hit a mine along the road to Zastino; the *Totenkopf* commander and his driver were seriously wounded. After his initial treatment, Eicke was transferred to a hospital at Lauderi, with his right hip, leg and foot full of fragments. Command of the division was then assigned temporarily to *SS-Staf.* Kleinheisterkamp, the officer with the most experience in the *Totenkopf*.

The next day, 7 July, *SS-Ostubaf.* Becker assumed command of *SS-Tot.Inf.Rgt.3.* To resume the attack against Sebesh, his regiment was reinforced by *II./SS-Tot.Inf.Rgt.1* of *SS-Stubaf.* Schulze. Meanwhile, *SS-Kampfgruppe "Simon"*, formed with the other two battalions of *SS-Tot.Inf.Rgt.1*, the *1.Kp./SS-T.Pz.Jg.-Abt.* and the *1.Kp./SS-T.Pi.-Btl.*, was sent to assault Durbrowka and Opotschka. The infantrymen of *I./SS-Tot.Inf.Rgt.1* led the attack against the enemy positions. In the afternoon the attack by the SS troops was once again stalled by the strong Soviet resistance. The enemy attempted to counterattack, using some tanks as well, but without much determination. That allowed the SS troops to enter the outskirts of

Opotschka towards nightfall, where they dug in soon afterwards in order to repel yet another enemy counterattack. Subjected to strong enemy pressure, the SS troops were finally forced to withdraw again, to as far as Max Simon's command post.

A *Pak 36* during an attack.

An *MG-34*, against Soviet positions on the *"Stalin Line"*.

SS-*Hstuf.* **Ruppmann (***Bundesarchiv***).**

The commander of *SS-Tot.Inf.Rgt.1* had meanwhile been ordered to hold his positions regardless of cost. Bitter defensive fighting ensued, with the SS soldiers fighting like devils, hanging on doggedly to their positions. In the end the Soviets were thrown back, but SS troop losses were high. The infantrymen of *SS-Tot.Inf.Rg.3* ran into serious difficulties in front of the Sebesh positions and also had to face violent counterattacks mounted by Soviet infantry. It was only after several hours that the SS troops managed to resume their advance, after neutralizing the enemy defensive positions.

Also on 8 July, the *Totenkopf* troops continued their attacks against the Stalin Line fortifications. The Soviets threw fresh troops into the battle and for the first time since the beginning of the campaign, the SS soldiers had to face massive numbers of tanks, in particular KV-1 and KV-2 types, whose armor was too thick to be penetrated by the 37 mm *Pak*. However, these tanks were heavy and not very maneuverable, making easy targets for the *Panzerjäger* who were able to immobilize them by firing at their tracks, then leaving it to the engineers to destroy them with magnetic mines. The fighting was ruthless. *II./SS-*

Tot.Inf.Rgt.3, which was attacking to the left of the railway line leading to Sebesh, suffered heavy losses, among which was the loss of its commander, *SS-Hstuf.* Ruppmann[3]. Command of the battalion was assumed by *SS-Hstuf.* Their[4]. Around 19:00, *SS-Tot.Inf.Rgt.3* was finally able to report to division headquarters that Sebesh had been captured. Support provided by an army assault gun battery was a determining factor.

The remains of a *KV-1* tank destroyed.

A *Totenkopf* artillery piece.

Totenkopf troops under Soviet artillery fire.

A 20 mm Flak piece being used against ground targets.

SS-Tot.Inf.Rgt.1 meanwhile still had not been able to get close to Opotschka, having had to deal with a counterattack by Soviet armor. *SS-Staf.* Simon was wounded during that fighting and was replaced as regimental commander by *SS-Ostubaf.* Becker, while command of *SS-Tot.Inf.Rgt.3* passed to Karl Hermann. The following day, *SS-Kampfgruppe "Hermann"*, consisting of *SS-Tot.Inf.Rgt.2* and *SS-Tot.Inf.Rgt.3*, was to attack from Sebesh towards Opotschka to go the aid of *SS-Kampfgruppe "Simon"*. The SS troops were able to get to the outskirts of Opotschka, only to find themselves surrounded by the enemy. Thanks to supporting fire from German artillery, the Soviet grip was broken and towards evening, after several hours of bitter fighting, *SS-Tot.Inf.Rgt.3* was able to re-establish contact with the division headquarters. On 10 July, *SS-Kampfgruppen "Simon"* and *"Hermann"* resumed their attack against Opotschka. *II./SS-Tot.Inf.Rgt.3* managed to circle the Soviet defenses from the west and to invest Opotschka from the north.

SS-Ostubaf. Becker, wounded in the shoulder, continues to remain in command.

"Stalin Line" bunkers captured by *Totenkopf* troops.

Totenkopf troops in the forest south of Opotschka.

Around 11:00, the city fell completely into the hands of the SS troops. It was a great success, but it cost the division 164 killed, 340 wounded and 34 missing. Since the beginning of the campaign on the Eastern Front, the division had suffered 490 killed (20 officers), 1,373 wounded (58 officers) and 34 missing. Many of the infantry companies were down to only about fifteen men fit for combat. It was because of these high losses that *SS-Tot.Inf.Rgt.1* and 3 were reinforced with personnel from *I.* and *II./SS-Tot.Inf.Rgt.2,* and the support companies of *SS-Tot.Inf.Rgt.2* were all disbanded. In any event, the Stalin Line, which was the first great obstacle along the road to Leningrad, had finally been breached and the Soviets were withdrawing to the northwest.

Notes

[1] Otto Baum, born on 15 November 1911 in Stetten-Hechingen, SS Number 237 056. He had served previously in *5./Sta. "Germania"* and following an officer's course at the *SS-Junkerschule* in Braunschweig he joined the *Leibstandarte* commanding *7./LSSAH.*

[2] Paul Monich, born on 26 March 1913 in Nuremberg, SS Number 120 904.

[3] Kurt Ruppmann, born on 29 December 1912 in Kirchheim-Teck, SS Number 105 642. He had served previously in *7./Sta. "Germania"* and in command of *12./SS-Tot.Inf.Rgt.3.*

[4] Karl Their, born on 10 June 1911 in Strasburg, SS Number 94 248. He had served previously as commander of *SS-Tot.Inf.Rgt.3.*

Bibliography

M. Afiero, "3.SS-Panzer-Division Totenkopf, vol.I – 1939-1943", Associazione Culturale Ritterkreuz

Karl Nicolussi-Leck
Italian Volunteer in the Waffen-SS
by Peter Mooney

SS-Ustuf. **Karl Nicolussi-Leck.**

SS-Stubaf. **Muhlenkamp.**

Born in Pfatten, Bozen, on the 14th of March 1917, then a region that was part of the Austro-Hungarian Empire. At the end of the war, that area moved to the control of Italy. Nicolussi-Leck's youth had a predominantly German 'feel' to it, but also one that was undergoing transformation by the new Italian rulers. By the late-1920s, all traces of the German influences were being banned and replaced with overt Italian ones, including Italian nationals moving into this area. He finished secondary school in late-July 1936, then in the autumn of the same year, began a three-year stint at university in Padua; he studied law and science there. In these pre-war years, he was active in the *Volkischer Kampfring Sudtirols*, a political organization that had a pro-German outlook and he was one of the prominent leaders. In the wartime images of Nicolussi-leck, you can see him wearing a Hitler Youth pin, which was given for his service in that organization, as he was never a member of the Hitler Youth itself. His increasing pro-German political leanings also ran parallel to the Italian and German negotiations, which resulted in the South Tyrol region being ceded to Italy by Adolf Hitler. Part of that agreement allowed for the resettlement of the pro-German population; Nicolussi-Leck was one of those. At the end of 1939, he opted to move to Germany and looked for a new outlet for his pro-German views; he found one in the shape of the SS. He volunteered for, and was accepted into the SS in early-1940, being given the SS Number 423 876. After his basic training, he was promoted to the rank of *SS-Rottenführer* and posted to the *SS-Regiment Deutschland*. With them, he went back southwards, only this time to the southeast, where he took part in the Balkans campaign. He had clearly showed aptitude early on, as by the time of his first military action, he had been promoted further and was holding *SS-Scharführer* rank. Remaining with *SS-Division Reich*, he was moved to the *SS-Regiment Der Führer* by the time of the invasion of the Soviet Union. He moved with that unit through central Russia, towards its capital. He had shown leadership qualities and was selected to to take part in an officer's preparatory course, following that by attending Bad Tolz between November 1941 and January 1942. He graduated there and was promoted to *SS-*

Untersturmführer on the 20th of April 1942. By then, he was with the *Panzer Regiment* within *SS-Division Wiking*, serving initially with the *2.Kompanie* who were equipped the *Panzer IVs*. This principal armoured unit of the *Waffen-SS* was being trained in Germany in early 1942, but in June they embarked for the southern reaches of the eastern front, with Nicolussi-Leck in tank number 221. The commanding officer for *Wiking's* Panzer Battalion was *SS-Sturmbannführer* Johannes Rudolf Muhlenkamp.

Panzer of *Wiking* marching, Summer 1942 (*U.S. NARA*).

A Wiking PzKpfw.III (NA).

In the Caucasus

In July 1942, they were advancing towards Rostov and the approach route is where Nicolussi-Leck engaged in this first armour-related actions; also his first for *Wiking*. His capabilities came to the fore during the engagements with their Soviet enemy and recognition quickly followed. The Second Class Iron Cross was awarded on the 25th of July, for actions in helping to push through to Rostov. That objective had been the scene for the *Leibstandarte's* attempts (where Heinrich Springer has earned his Knight's Cross) the previous November, but this time, the Heer's *13.Panzer Division* captured the objective. The push into the Caucausus region was now the order of the day and Nicolussi-Leck's actions at Krapotkin, north of the Kuban River, earned him the First Class Iron Cross, on the 9th of August. The Black Wound Badge was approved on the 2nd of September and the Tank Assault Badge on the 11th. He continued to lead his platoon as they advanced against the determined enemy, knocking out enemy positions along the way, and earning an increasingly good reputation as a daring and capable tank commander. He was known also for his development of effective tactics and even penned a training manual on these.

In late-September they were fighting for the objective of Sagopschin and during that battle, Nicolussi-Leck's tank was hit and disabled, although all of the crew baled out and survived. Into October and Malgobek came under the control of the soldiers from *Wiking*. On the 15th of that month, Nicolussi-Leck was given command of the *1.Kompanie*, due to the combat loss of many of the *1.Kompanie's* former commanders. The enemy were providing very stiff resistance and his objective at the head of his *Kompanie*, was Hill 701. That target fell to his men and they accounted for many enemy tanks and infantry, as well as other equipment. The defense of that hill had only begun though and during that heavy fighting, Nicolussi-Leck was shot in the arm, after bailing out of his tank, which was hit and began to smoke. That wound resulted in him being moved to Germany for the required treatment.

A Wiking PzKpfw.III in the Malgobeck's sector (Giorgio Bussano Collection).

Panzer '311' of the 3.Kp./SS-Pz.Abt.5 in the Malgobeck's sector.

A railway transport of *Panther* tanks for Nicolussi-Leck's 8.*Kompanie*.

SS-Gruf. Gille at work in his command post at Kovel.

When the *Wiking* went on the attack in the west of Kovel, the region was still covered with snow. In the photo, the advance of the *Panther*s along the Lublin-Kovel railway line (*Trang*).

The Battle for Kovel

It took him around six-months to be declared fit for duty and once he was, he remained in Germany and was sent to the newly raised II Battalion, within *Wiking*'s *Panzer Regiment*; they were being formed in Grafenwohr in the summer of 1943. He became the Commander of the 8.*Kompanie* and in November 1943, he was promoted to *SS-Obersturmführer*. As their training neared its end, in January 1944, they were equipped with *Panther* tanks. Whilst he was in Germany, the Soviets advances had continued westwards and his previous location of the Caucausus has long been back under their control. This Soviet enemy pushed across the Dnjepr and almost destroyed *Wiking* (and other units) within the Tscherkassy Pocket. Four hundred miles to the northwest of there, they would surround the location of Kovel. Inside there was *Wiking*'s enigmatic commander, *SS-Gruppenführer* Herbert-Otto Gille. He stood there with five-thousand German troops and civilians and any attempts up to that point to free them from their enemy encirclement, had failed. During the closing few days of March, *SS-Obersturmführer* Nicolussi-Leck arrived at the positions of the *Wiking* Division, who were outside the besieged city. In conference with the senior commanders, he was tasked with leading the push towards the encircled location. What unfolded next, has passed into legend and it was evidence of the character of this soldier. He started the push on the 27th of March and his initial force of seventeen *Panthers* met fierce resistance near Czerkasy. The ground was not favourable to these forty-five ton metal beasts and five of them became stuck fast in the thick mud. Nicolussi-Leck used them to provide supporting fire to the remaining, advancing tanks; they were also advancing in snow flurries, which reduced visibility considerably. Three more Panthers fell victim to the enemy defensive fire. Pausing later in the afternoon, the stuck tanks were freed by recovery vehicles, which bolstered their attacking potency. That was reduced not long after, when the advance attempts resumed.

SS-Grenadiers **and a** *Panther* **tank during the attack against Kovel.**

Wiking Panthers **in Kovel area.**

Heavy fire and soft ground reduced the force to only eight tanks. They finally reached Czerkasy in the evening and took control of it. Nicolussi-Leck increased his strength during the night, with some of the immobilized tanks being freed and sent forward, but also from captured equipment; they were now only around six to seven miles from Kovel. The main objective of Kovel was still to be reached and that advance started the next morning, the 30th of March. At the start of the push, a radio message was sent through, ordering him not to advance and abandon the attempt. Nicolussi-Leck told his radio operator to relay a reply that he had been unable to find him. By making this decision, Nicolussi-Leck was disobeying a direct order, but also instructing one of his men to do the same thing. His rationale for doing this was that he felt the trapped soldiers and civilians' need was too great to ignore, he therefore pushed onwards towards Kovel with his nine remaining *Panther* tanks. As they moved forwards, two of the lead tanks hit mines and lost their tracks.

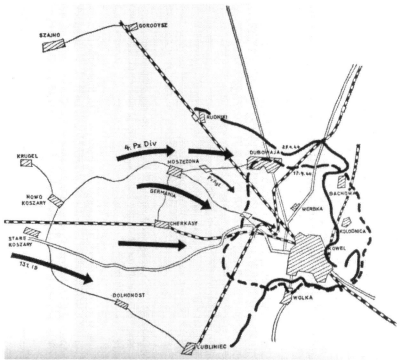

Operations in the Kovel sector, April 1944.

SS-Obersturmführer **Nicolussi-Leck.**

They were ordered to defend where they stood, as the commander carried on with the remaining seven Panthers. Those two tanks would be subjected to fierce enemy attacks throughout the 30th of March, as Nicolussi-Leck advanced eastwards. His advance continued and just outside of Kovel, they met further enemy resistance, which was dealt with. At that point, he was asked to halt the advance by the accompanying Heer infantry, something he chose to ignore; he had a clear objective in his mind and nothing was stopping him! After clearing the above enemy resistance, he came across friendly troops for the first time and at that point, knew he had succeeded in breaking the ring around Kovel. At just after 08:00 hours, he finally reached the command post of *SS-Gruppenführer* Herbert-Otto Gille. On the route to reach his Divisional Commander, Nicolussi-Leck and his Kompanie succeeded in knocking out 16 anti-tank guns, 2 anti-aircraft guns, 2 tanks, 40 anti-tank rifles, as well as quantities of mortars and other enemy weapons. Alongside this, none of the tanks that were immobilized during the advance, were total losses; the skills of the workshops returned them to full service soon after. His advance and decisions made along the way, which included ignoring orders, resulted in the opening of an enemy encirclement surrounding Kovel.

Panther 813 of the 8.Kp / SS-Pz.Abt. 5.

Soldiers of *131.Inf.Div.* and a *Panther* of *Wiking*, April 1944.

He thereby removed another potential disaster for the Germans, at a time when they were under extreme pressure from the enemy. His accomplishments did not go unnoticed and the very next day, his Battalion Commander, Johannes Muhlenkamp, penned a recommendation for the award of the Knight's Cross to Karl Nicolussi-Leck; that short recommendation read as follows: '...SS-Ostuf. *Nicolussi-*

Leck has, on the 29.3.1944, as the leader of the 8./SS-Panzer-Regiment Wiking, penetrated into Czerkasy with his Panther Kompanie, *and under the most difficult of ground conditions. This was despite established and strong enemy positions occupying 8 Km West of Kovel, which destroyed numerous vehicles. On the 30.3.1944, Nicolussi-Leck made the decision to advance at 04:15 hours from Czerkasy, along the road and then the railway line from Maciejow to Kovel. During fighting against enemy tanks, Kovel was reached with 7* Panthers. *He has thus brought a decisive reinforcement to the position of Kovel and on the same day, shot up 17 enemy tanks in Kovel.'*

Panther '823' marching along the railway line, April 1944.

SS-Obersturmführer Nicolussi-Leck.

To this was added the thoughts of *SS-Standartenführer* Richter on the 2nd April: *'...This recommendation is warmly agreed with. SS-Obersturmführer Nicolussi-Leck has, through his surprise advance with 7 Panthers, done under his own initiative, broken into Kovel. He thereby significantly strengthened the position of Kovel. He has distinguished himself through his exemplary, personal bravery.'*

SS-Gruppenfuhrer Gille added his thoughts on the 3rd of April: *'Through the successful, independent and bold advance of SS-Obersturmführer Nicolussi-Leck, the strength of Fortress Kovel, who had been trapped for 3-weeks, was decisively reinforced. I especially agree with this proposal for the brave SS-Leader.'*

This request was approved on the 9th of April 1944. Nicolussi-Leck was very unassuming in his reaction to this award then, plus in the conversations I had with him after the war. He was focused on his task and nothing was going to stop him. He done his job, despite this being against orders, as his desire to rescue the trapped and wounded Germans in Kovel was too important – something he was prepared to sacrifice himself for, both in action and in career. He mentioned to me that his actual award arrived as part of the supply drops into the city and Gille presented it to him personally. I am not aware of any photos of this event, as the force inside was small and no photographers were on hand!

SS-Ostuf. Nicolussi-Leck in his turret.

SS-Obersturmführer Nicolussi-Leck.

Ostuf. Nicolussi-Leck in his turret.

In the intervening days since he managed to get inside to Kovel, the situation for the soldiers there was far from over. The enemy managed to once again close the ring around this location, with Nicolussi-Leck's tanks providing a much-needed strengthening role for Gille and the other defenders there. The Germans were busy moving further troops towards this location and fighting continued inside and outside the encirclement, in the opening days of April 1944. For four days, Nicolussi-Leck and his small group of Panthers became part of the trapped troops and civilians inside Kovel. They were continuously attacked by the Soviets and losses mounted to his tank squad. In the evening of the 4th of April, Muhlenkamp led the remaining *Wiking* tanks into Kovel and therefore, decisively broke the enemy hold there; larger Heer forces moved into Kovel too. Together, they focused on enlarging the areas under their control and clearing out enemy strongpoints that had arisen within the confines of the city itself. They remained there until the 8th of May, when the *Panzer Regiment* was withdrawn from the city of Kovel and placed as armoured reserve for the *LVI Pz.Korps*, west of Kovel. They remained there as the major Soviet offensive opened on the 22nd of June 1944. The enemy hit Army Group Centre with a superiority in strength of five-to-one. Part of these moves by the enemy, arrived north and south of Kovel around the 7th of July.

Wiking's Panther **marching, Summer 1944.**

SS-Ostuf. **Nicolussi-Leck in his *Panther '801'.***

Nicolussi-Leck and his men fought once again there. A huge enemy armoured force of an estimated 400 tanks flowed past the positions of the *Wiking* panzers. They waited for the opportune moment, then opened fire. In less than one hour, over 100 enemy tanks were destroyed, with many more limping back eastwards in the relative cover of the forests nearby. The reports from Muhlenkamp were initially met with disbelief, until they were verified by a visual count of the destroyed vehicles. That blunting of the enemy attempts in this area, allowed a little respite, but for the *Wiking* panzer men, they were withdrawn around 175 miles north into Poland, around the Bialystok area. He continued to lead his *8.Kompanie* through the battles of summer 1944, mainly around Warsaw, where they inflicted more losses on the Soviet armour, but this was not enough to reverse the tide of the war. Nicolussi-Leck was wounded again in early-October, which resulted in another temporary removal from the front. He returned in December and just prior to that, had been given command of the *II.Battalion, SS-Panzer Regiment 5*, in mid-November 1944; bear in mind that he was still only holding the rank of *SS-Obersturmführer!*

Nicolussi-Leck and his *Panther '800' (Mooney).*

SS-Ostuf. Nicolussi-Leck talking with *SS-Hstuf.* Fritz Hannes, Summer 1944 (*Charles Trang*).

On the Hungarian front

At the end of December, *Wiking* were ordered over 550 miles southwest towards Hungary, to help relieve the trapped troops there. They arrived west of the city and engaged enemy troops almost immediately. Within four days, they had fought to within 20 miles of Budapest, but lacked the overall strength to get any further within the enemy ring around the Hungarian capital. In the middle of the second week, they were moved 25 miles north to Estergom, to begin another relief attempt on the besieged city. Nicolussi-Leck led his Battalion as part of that overall attack and within two days, they had got within a dozen miles of Budapest. At that stage, they were moved again, this time 75 miles southwest to Veszprem, near Lake Balaton! Their next attempt was to reach Budapest from the south and that got underway during the third week of that month. That advance took them around 60 miles east to Adony on the Danube River, less than 40 miles from the centre of Budapest. These various attempts came to nothing for *Wiking* and they lost many good men along the way. The enemy strength was growing and they launched a major offensive at the end of January, which resulted in *Wiking* having to move westwards, whilst in contact with the hotly pursuing enemy! They reached an area 25 miles west of Adony, where they found temporary respite. For Karl Nicolussi-Leck, he was about to engage in another '*legendary*' mission! A promotion to *SS-Hauptsturmführer* for him, took place back on on the 30th of January 1945. This *Wiking* Battalion commander was tasked with travelling northwards into Germany, with the mission to collect new tanks, urgently needed to replace the *Wiking* losses suffered in the recent heavy fighting.

The German Cross in Gold

He began that journey in March, which was the same month that he was awarded the German Cross in Gold. The recommendation for that was written by *SS-Ostubaf.* Fritz Darges on the 7th of January and was approved on the 10th of March; awarded for the following:

SS-Obersturmführer **Nicolussi-Leck.**

'…SS-Obersturmführer *Nicolussi-Leck has been a leader of the panzer-arm of the I./SS-Panzer-Regiment 5 on the 1.3.1942 as a Platoon leader, and since 1.4.43 as a commander of a* Panther Kompanie. *His great inner enthusiasm for the panzer-arm and his innate momentum, coupled with a selfless willingness to act, has led him to great achievements with his* Panther Kompanie. *In all crises, he has especially preserved himself through the selfless use of his own person and prudent leadership of the* Kompanie. *Nicolussi-Leck is a holder of the Knight's Cross of the Iron Cross, which was awarded to him on 15.4.44.*

1.) On the 07.07.1944, Nicolussi-Leck's Kompanie was deployed in a counterattack against the town of Kruhel and the hill west of it. Due to the Russian occupation of Kruhel and the elevated terrain, the infantry Division operating to the north, near Smydin, was endangered. Nicolussi-Leck's Kompanie ran into a strong front of anti-tank guns that had been established southwest of Kruhel and initially got tied down in a firefight. Swinging out to the north, he was able to attack the flank of the anti-tank gun front in an agile push, while simultaneously tying it down from the front. At the same moment, the opponent attacked Nicolussi-Leck's Kompanie with seven T-34s. Acting on his own decision and with relentless personal effort, while personally leading the way for the Kompanie, he attacked the enemy tanks and knocked out six. With lightening-quick action, the anti-tank guns were destroyed in the process. After this, the opponent ceased his attacks into our retreat area movements. The infantry forces operating in the Smydin area could disengage as ordered and without a flank threat.

2.) On the 23.07.1944, Nicolussi-Leck was ordered to attack and take the town of Czeremcha and Hill 181.2., north of it, employing his Kompanie without any infantry support. Securing against all sides, Nicolussi-Leck pushed towards Czeremcha through the difficult forest and swampy terrain. The enemy infantry withdrew to the north. Travelling at high speed, eight enemy tanks and assault guns pushed into Czeremcha from the east, before the town could be taken. In a series of fierce armoured duels, Nicolussi-Leck's Kompanie destroyed two SU-85s, two T-43s and six T-34s. After all enemy tanks had been knocked out, Nicolussi-Leck pushed onto Kleszczele. Acting on his own decision and without prudent leadership, he established contact with the 4.Pz.Div. attacking from the north. Major groups of enemy forces were cut off and could be systematically destroyed in the subsequent battles.

Nicolussi-Leck in a *Kubelwagen*.

3.) On the 04.08.1944, in the area of Okuniew, the opponent managed to break the connection that had been established between 'Wiking' and the Warsaw bridgehead. The Kompanie, led by Nicolussi-Leck and some elements of an Armoured Personnel Carrier Battalion, were ordered to overcome the stubbornly resisting opponent and re-establish contact. At the first light of dawn on the 05.08.1944, Nicolussi-Leck pushed in the direction of Okuniew. Having the advantage of fog and rainy weather, Nicolussi-Leck was able to destroy an anti-tank gun front set up on the boundary of the forest near Michalow, from a short distance. In a dashing advance, he pushed into the enemy infantry to good effect. Nicolussi-Leck made it possible to free some of our elements that had been temporarily encircled in the area east of the bridgehead. In the process, three enemy tanks were captured while one T-43 and two self-propelled guns were knocked out.

4.) On the 13.10.1944, the Panzer-Aufklarungs Abteilung 5 *and the* I./SS-Panzer Regiment 5 *were ordered, at 14:00 hours, to withdraw from the forest northwest of Nieporet, past the crossroads south of Zagrobi and, together with the* I./Germania, *occupy the railway embankment up to the cemetery northeast of K.-Wieliszew. Strong armour-supported enemy infantry forces had broken through towards Wieliszew, reaching the cemetery towards the northeast. Realising the danger to the entire divisional sector caused by this,* SS-Obersturmführer *Nicolussi-Leck regrouped and subsequently led them on a counterattack against the western boundary of the forest at K.-Wieliszew, by then, occupied by the Russians. In co-operation with our tanks, the opponent was forced back to the cemetery after a fierce struggle and a further breakthrough was prevented.* SS-Obersturmführer *Nicolussi-Leck is a model Panzer-leader. He is personally able to combine a dashing and tactical approach. He has mastered all the situations and led his* Kompanie *to great achievements. I consider Nicolussi-Leck to be particularly worthy of the German Cross in Gold.'*

On the same document, was an additional endorsement from his Divisional Commander, SS-*Standartenführer* Karl Ullrich, who highlighted Nicolussi-Leck's special bravery and capabilities; he too stated that he felt that he was especially worthy of this award. Around one week later, his former Divisional Commander and now commander of the *IV.SS-Panzer Korps*, (now *SS-Obergruppenführer*) Herbert Otto Gille, added his own endorsement to this recommendation, giving it his warmest approval; it was officially approved on the 10th of March 1945. With that added to his tunic, giving recognition of his further achievements over eight months earlier, Nicolussi-Leck's focus was on his current orders, that of collecting the new tanks. They arrived in the first few days of April, initially in the Gutersloh area, and elements almost immediately ran into parts of the British *6th Airbourne Division*. They had no vehicles at that stage, but soon acquired 13 armoured halftracks. They then made their way towards Hannover, where their arrival coincided with the arrival of strong American forces in the shape of the *U.S. 84th Infantry Division* and the *771st Armoured Battalion*. The *Wiking* men took up defensive positions within the city of Hannover in agreement with the city Commandant and began to engage the enemy. They knocked out some of the enemy tanks by using *Panzerfausts*, one of the tanks falling victim to Nicolussi-Leck personally; an act like that would have normally earned him the single-handed tank destruction badge, but the 'official channels' were notably absent then!

A German *Jagdpanther* engaged in combat.

Jagdpanther **abandoned by Germans, April 1945.**

On the 8th of April 1945, Nicolussi-Leck learned of some available tanks in a nearby factory, from locals. He took a small detachment and went to the location. Not knowing what to expect, their visit there netted them seven brand new *JagdPanther* tank destroyers, a 'gift' that left them speechless initially! The addition of these very potent vehicles bolstered his small Battlegroup, and they felt ready to halt the American advance in this area.

Nicolussi-Leck and me.

After some final preparations on the vehicles, including sighting the main guns, filling up with ammunition and fuel supplies, they set off to take on their much stronger enemy. Over the next few days, this Battlegroup operated around the Hannover and Celle areas, with the Americans being under the impression that they were up against a full German Panzer Division. The reality was seven *JagdPanthers* and thirteen halftracks under *SS-Hauptsturmführer* Nicolussi-Leck. They did slowly lose some of their vehicles to the enemy, but along the way, they succeeded in destroying dozens of American tanks and many other enemy vehicles. Karl Nicolussi-Leck was captured in the course of this fighting, on the 22nd of April 1945, bringing his war to an end, but starting three years as a prisoner of war. He was awarded the Silver Wound Badge during the war, but the exact date is not listed. Some sources state that he was wounded five times; Nicolussi-Leck stated to me personally, a total of four wounds, two light and two heavy. During the fighting itself, he had briefly taken prisoners, but released these within a day or so. One of them was a young American Lieutenant named Albert Robbins. This former American soldier made contact with Nicolussi-Leck in 1980, to determine if he was the same *Waffen-SS* soldier he recalled in this fighting at the end of the war and someone whom he personally attributed to saving his life during the fighting! He was indeed and both men corresponded and met up many times over the intervening years. After being released from prisoner or war detention, he returned to northern Italy. He began to build a life for himself, but also focused on helping others. In the decades after the war, he helped establish training and education facilities, which benefited and trained many people; these facilities also helped the local area. He was also a patron of the arts and helped many artists pursue their passion. When I visited him in 2003, his house and surrounding grounds contained many of these works of art. Karl Nicolussi-Leck, the former *Waffen-SS Hauptsturmführer*, Battalion Commander, holder of the Silver Wound Badge, German Cross in Gold and Knight's Cross, died at the end of August 2008. He personally supported my 'Waffen-SS Knight's Cross' book project and I am honoured to have had the chance to personally meet him. I hope you have enjoyed this insight into a very effective combat soldier and European volunteer from the ranks of the *Waffen-SS*.

Bibliography
Personal face to face interview with Karl Nicolussi-Leck, 2003
Written correspondence with Karl Nicolussi-Leck, 2001-2008
Peter Strassner, "*European Volunteers, 5 SS Panzer Division Wiking*", J.J.Fedorowicz Publishing Ltd., 1998.
J.P. Moore, "*Führerliste Der Waffen-SS, Parts 1 to 4*", J.P.Moore Publishing, 2003.
P. Mooney, "*Waffen-SS Knights and Their Battles - Volume 4, January to May 1944*", Schiffer Publishing Ltd. 2016

The "MONTEROSA" Alpine Division of the R.S.I.
Alpine History of the "Iron Division!"
by Carlo Cucut

After the meetings between Mussolini and Hitler, followed by those between Graziani, Rahn and Wolf, and which were formally agreed to with the subsequent Buehle-Canevari Protocol, concerning the new Army of the Italian Social Republic, work was allowed to begin on the establishment of the four new Italian Divisions, trained, armed, and structured similar to the *Wehrmacht* divisions. One of the four divisions was to be an alpine division. Thus, on January 1, 1944, the 4th Alpine Division "*Monterosa*" was officially established at the Centro Costituzione Grandi Unità (Large Unit Formation Center) of Vercelli with recruits from the classes of 1924 and 1925, who in mid-February reached the Heuberg, Feldstetten and Munsingen training camps, as well as those soldiers who, in October 1943, had formed a training Battalion which former internees had also joined. Also included as part of the division were all of those alpine units that were located outside of Italy on September 8, 1943, and which had joined the RSI and had been transferred to Munsingen.

A 75/1 Skoda howitzer of the "Aosta" Artillery Group being towed by a mule.

These were the "*Exilles*" Battalion of the 3rd Alpine Regiment commanded by Lt. Col.. Armando Farinacci, which came from Montenegro; the 15th Artillery Regiment, coming from Albania; the alpini of the Group of Alpine Battalions "*Valle*" ("*Val Leogra*" and "*Val Pescara*" battalions and the "*Valle Isonzo*" Artillery Group with the 37th and 38th mountain artillery batteries), from Greece; elements of the XX Ski Group from France. These were the units that constituted the framework of the "*Monterosa*" Division. In the training camps a rigorous training period began according to the techniques used in the German Army under the constant and diligent control of the German instructors belonging to *1.Gebirsjäger Division*, veterans of the campaigns of Norway, Greece, the Balkans and the Caucasus.

Munsingen 1944: an Alpini squad during combat training.

Battalion transport vehicles of the Liaison Battalion.

This was a totally new type of training even for those Italians who were professional soldiers or who had previous combat experience, carried out under all climatic conditions and with few rest periods. In only six months of hard work, compared to the period of training for German recruits which normally lasted for a period of at least a year, training of the Italian units was completed, equipment was issued and a respectable degree of unit integration was achieved. The training of the "*Monterosa*" alpine division represents the most intense training ever experienced by a large Italian unit. Intense and conducted in accordance with the rigid and effective standards of the *Wehrmacht*, the same basic training was applied to Italian military personnel; officers, NCOs, veterans and young recruits were all subjected to the same type and level of training.

Munsingen, July 1944: Italian 'Alpini' in training with a *MG-42*.

Munsingen, July 1944: Italian 'Alpini' with a German instructor.

From the beginning, everything was planned in the smallest detail and divided into phased training sessions designed to provide the Italian military with more and more specialized training levels; beginning with basic infantry training, it it progressed to specialized training, preparing the men to operate under all operational conditions and at the same time to excel in the specific duties peculiar to the alpine, grenadier and *Bersaglieri* troops. The entire training cycle took place in the Munsingen, Heuberg and Feldstetten camps in Baden Wuttemberg. On 16 July, the *"Monterosa"* Division, drawn up in its entirety on the Gansevach plain, was reviewed by the Duce, who, after a warm speech, handed over the combat banners to the regiments. Immediately after the ceremony, units began moving to Italy, which they reached in the second half of July with railway convoys frequently attacked by Allied air raids.

Munsingen 17 July 1944: the *Duce* visit the *Monterosa*. At his right, General Mario Carloni.

Munsingen, 1944: Alpini of the *Monterosa* during a ceremony.

From 19 to 26 July 1944, 627 officers and 19,325 officers and troops departing on thirty-seven trains were processed through the Domegliara railway station. Returning to Italy, the "*Monterosa*" was deployed in Liguria, joining the '*Armata Liguria*' under the command of Maresciallo Graziani, an

Army consisting of Italian and German units deployed or waiting to be deployed from St. Bernard in the Valle d 'Aosta to La Spezia, with the task of defending the Ligurian coast, and then the Western Alps, in the event of an Allied landing in Liguria. The division's first commander was Colonel Umberto Manfredini, followed by General Goffredo Ricci, then General Mario Carloni, and finally Colonel Giorgio Milazzo.

General Mario Carloni.

The "Monterosa" in Liguria

The first units of the division arrived in Liguria around 23/24 July, moving to the Levante Riviera, where they relieved the German units of the *42.Jäger-Division*. In early August the deployment of the *"Monterosa"* was completed. The defensive sector assigned to the division went from Nervi to Levanto, included, and was subdivided into two regimental sub-sectors: the 1st Alpine Regiment sector ran from Nervi to Sestri Levante (with Sestri Levante itself excluded), and apportioned the area among its three Battalions: *"Aosta"* (from Nervi to Portofino) - *"Bassano"* (from Portofino to Zoagli) - *"Intra"* (from Zoagli to Sestri Levante); the 2nd Alpine Regiment sector ran from Sestri Levante to Levanto, with the following battalions:

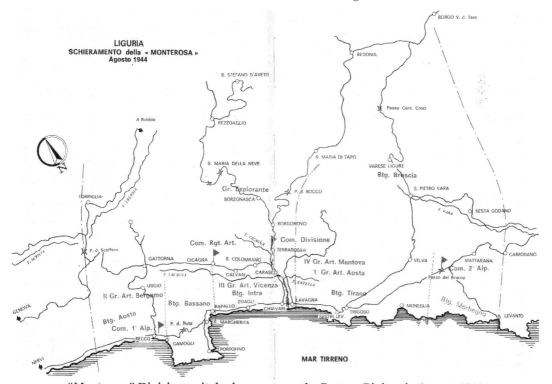

"Monterosa" **Division unit deployments on the Eastern Riviera in August 1944.**

"*Tirano*" (from Sestri to Moneglia) - "*Morbegno*" (from Moneglia to Levanto) - "*Brescia*" (in reserve at Passo del Bracco); the 1st Alpine Artillery Regiment divided its groups in support of the two regiments: Gr. "*Bergamo*" (south of Uscio in support of *1st Rgt.*) - Gr. "*Aosta*" (at Casarza in support of the *2nd Rgt.*) - Gr. "*Vicenza*" (in Campodonico) - Gr. *"Mantova"* (at Coreglia). The division headquarters was deployed to Terracossa in Carasco, retaining the reconnaissance group (at Borzonasca) as the divisional reserve, the engineer battalion (in Carasco, minus two companies deployed with the two regiments for the initial fortification work), the "*Ivrea*" reserve battalion (in Borgonuovo) and the transportation battalion (in the area of Cicagna). Also in Cicagna were the two medical units.

Italy, August 1944: A unit of the 1st Alpine Artillery Rgt. in marching toward the operation zone.

Garfagnana: *Bersagliere* **of the '***Gruppo Cadelo***'.**

The territorial boundaries of the division were: the Nervi-Bobbio border on the western side and the Levanto-Borgotaro border on the eastern side, for a depth of about thirty kilometers, crossing the Apennine watershed on the Emilian side. The "*Monterosa*" units took possession of preexisting positions, which were somewhat spread out and weak in places, and built new ones, greatly improving the existing thin line of defense by integrating it with new positions for machine gun, mortars and cannons. The experience of the landings that had been carried out by the Allies in Europe had shown that such a strong enemy had no problem to force a defensive line along the coast. The division then developed a new defensive plan, approved by both the German headquarters and Maresciallo Graziani, which called for only small early warning and rapid response units to guard the coastline, with the strength of a company or little more, supported by existing fortifications.

Italian-French border, Autumn 1944, Alpini of the *Monterosa* on the march of transfer.

Ligurian Apennines, Autumn 1944: Alpino of the *Monterosa*.

The main defense then moved to an inner line running from Uscio to Carrodano, passing through Carasco, Passo del Bracco and Mattarana, that is, along the first hills that dominate the coastal strip, and there the battalions set up strongpoints. In the event that this line was breached, a second defensive line was planned along the Apennine passes. The aim was to contain the enemy as much as possible, preventing him from coming into the Po Valley. Although the defense of the coast and of the countryside was the main purpose of the *"Monterosa"*, the other task that became increasingly important was the safety of roads and supply lines, with the control of the roads that led to the Po Valley, passing through the narrow Ligurian valleys and descending towards Piacenza.

Ligurian Riviera, September 1944: anti-aircraft position of the *Monterosa* Division.

Ligurian Riviera: Alpino of the *Monterosa* with the *MG-42*.

In the Ligurian hinterland there were numerous and fierce partisan formations, which, shortly after the arrival of the apine units, as early as July 26, began actions aimed at encouraging desertions, as well as carrying out numerous ambushes and attacks on isolated and numerically weak outposts. The *Alpini* were not prepared for civil war, they did not know about the partisans and had not been trained in guerrilla warfare, they were certain that they were going to go to the front to fight the Allied invaders, and instead they found themselves faced with other Italians who struck them from behind, incited them to betray their fellow soldiers, and attacked them while they were on leave. It was an abrupt and tragic awakening, which involved mourning and tragedy for both fronts, not counting the civilians who were involved through no fault of their own. The control of the territory, in order to cope with the flare-up of partisan activity, forced the command of the *"Monterosa"* to create numerous lightly manned garrisons and detachments that were difficult to supply. The decision was made to set up several alarm companies, taking men from the various battalions; these companies were then grouped into two independent battalions, the "*Vestone*" and the "*Saluzzo*", which had the task of exercising control over the road network. This arrangement was found to be totally unsatisfactory, as the units did not conform to a standard organization type, lacked cohesion and were not well integrated with each other, all of which proved to have such a negative result that the Btg. "*Saluzzo*" was dissolved and the Btg. "*Vestone*" was instead plagued by a mass desertion that affected half the unit. In mid-August, under orders of the *'Armata Liguria'*, a grouping formed by several units of the division, designated the '*Colonna Farinacci*' (Farinacci column) after the name of its commander, carried out a rear area security operation involving about 2,500 men, which, advancing along the roads leading to the Po Valley, reached the inland towns and cleared the road network. Meanwhile, the landing that had been expected in Liguria took place in France, in Provence, thus making Liguria a secondary front and releasing forces to strengthen the other active fronts: the Gothic Line and the Western Alps.

A group of Alpini at the command of the division in Terrarossa, in Liguria.

The "*Monterosa*" Division was then disbanded and ceased to be an organic division, its units would be deployed on all three fronts until the end of the conflict. Remaining in Liguria, in defense of the coast and communications routes, from October 1944 to February 1945, were the Headquarters of the 2nd Regiment, the Btg. "*Morbegno*", the Btg. "*Ivrea*", the Btg. "*Aosta*" (less than the 1st Company), the Gr. Art. "*Aosta*", concentrated in the coastal stretch between Chiavari and Levanto, with the bulk of its forces further inland to defend the passes and road junctions at Bocco, Bracco, Forcella, and whose command was entrusted to Colonel Roscioli, the Deputy Commander of the division. With the departure of some of these units for Piedmont and the return of those deployed in Garfagnana, in March, the following elements of the division Departments were in Liguria: Headquarters of the 1ˢᵗ Alpine Regiment, with the 101ˢᵗ Anti-tank Company of and the Light Column, the "*Ivrea*" Battalion, the "*Cadelo*" Reconnaissance Group and the 1ˢᵗ Artillery Group "*Aosta*".

Autumn 1944: Alpini on the march towards a new destination in Piedmont.

"*Monterosa*" Division unit deployments on the Western Alps.

The "Monterosa" on the Western Alps

On August 15, 1944, when the "*Monterosa*" was deployed on the Ligurian coast for about twenty days, the Allies began Operation Anvil / Dragon, landing in French Provence between Toulon and Cannes, starting the advance northward along the valley of the Rhône. The advance of the French-American troops was rapid and threatened the Italian-French border area. At the beginning of September, the advance had already reached and crossed the Tinea Valley and continued with little opposition to Briancon and Chambery. The German command quickly reacted to the threat that would allow the Allies to cross the Alps and to move down to Piedmont and the Po Valley. The sparse garrison forces behind the Western Alps, usually units of the G.N.R. and the Black Brigades, which were busy mostly defending against the partisans rather than against regular units, were soon joined by the *LXXV.Armee-Korps*, consisting of the 34th Infantry Division and the 5th German Alpine Division, to which were added units of the "*Monterosa*" Division and later of the "*Littorio*" Division, as well as other independent units. The "*Monterosa*" battle group, designated the "Farinacci Group" (*Kampfgruppe Farinacci* - for the Germans), after the name of its commander, was made up of the *Bassano* and *Tirano* Battalions, as well as the *Vicenza* Artillery Group. Between September 9 and 15, the transfer to Piedmont began. The headquarters of the group was established in Saluzzo, with its logistical bases at Pinerolo and Borgo San Dalmazzo, while the units were split up and parceled out to the provinces of Cuneo and Turin. The "*Bassano*" Battalion was deployed between the Valli Varaita and Maira, with its headquarters in Casteldelfino and three companies in Val Varaita, while the other two companies went to Acceglio in Val Maira.

Troops of the "*Monterosa*" assembled at Torino during a ceremony in the winter of 1944/45.

A 75/40 anti-tank gun deployed on the Western Alps front.

On September 20, the transfer was completed and the by the 25th, all the hills, between Maddalena and Monviso, colle dell'Agnello, S. Véran, Longet, Auratet, and Maurin, were in the hands of the alpini, which after some fighting, they had recaptured from the *maquis* and partisans. Along this line, with a height varying between 2,500 and 2,800 meters, shelters, defensive positions and winter accommodations were built that allowed the battalion to remain in possession of until the end of the war. Operational activity against the French was limited, due to the particularly harsh winter, to patrol actions and artillery exchanges, and it was only with the approach of spring that military activity increased. This activity began with offensive actions by alpine patrols in the Tinea Valley and

Ubaye Valley, followed by French company-level attacks against the hills of S.Véran and dell'Agnello, both beaten back with strong losses to the attackers. But by then it was mid-April and the conflict was rapidly coming to an end. In early September the pack-mounted "*Vicenza*" Artillery Group was transferred to Valle Stura, where it relieved German units. The headquarters element was placed in Argentera and the batteries, in defense of the Colle della Maddalena, were emplaced in French territory: the 7th in Val Lanzargner, the 8th in the Rio du Pis Valley, and the 9th in Val Puriac, from where it had to relocate to Ferriere because the enemy batteries at Barcelonette had spotted it and taken it under fire. With the arrival of snow, the group was deployed to its winter quarters: the headquarters was established at Sambuco near Pietraporzio, the 7th and 8th Batteries were deployed to Colle della Maddalena and established positions in the valley, and the 9th went to S. Bernolfo. At the beginning of April 1945, *"Vicenza"* was ordered to move to Val Varaita and Val Maira, in support of the "*Bassano*" Battalion. Preparations had already begun and the billeting parties were already in place but the rapid turn of events prevented the transfer.

January 1945, Alpine Front: Maresciallo Rodolfo Graziani, commander of the '*Armata Liguria*' talks to officers and soldiers of the *Monterosa* Division.

The "*Tirano*" Battalion left Liguria on 9 September, arriving in Cesana (Torino Province) on September 11th. On September 13, it entered the line by relieving German units of the 85th Regiment of the *5.Gebirgs-Division 'Gams'*, to which it was tactically subordinated.

January 1945, Western Front: an Alpine Patrol in action.

It was deployed in an area that ran at altitudes above 2,000 meters, from Claviere passing through Rocca Clary and Punta Rascià to Mount Gimont, with the last combat position at Monte Chenaillet at 2,650 meters. The battalion headquarters was placed on the line at Punta Rascià, while the rear base remained in Pinerolo, Cesana became the advanced base and Bousson became the area for the company that in turn came down from the front line for its rest period. Towards mid-October, the French carried out a surprise raid and occupied the Chenaillet outpost, which was promptly re-occupied by a joint action of the "*Tirano*" alpine troops and the Germans, who, on the 21st, used a pincer movement to overcome the French defenders, a colonial unit. During that action, falling at the head of the attacking forces was an alpine trooper named Renato Assante, an Italian born in Turkey who had maintained Italian citizenship and who had come to Italy to enroll as a volunteer, joining the R.S.I. Army after the September 8 armistice and in whose memory the M.O.V.M. (Gold Medal for Military Valor) would be awarded. A new action took place on December 23, when a *Tirano* ski patrol along with German ski troops carried out a raid against the enemy lines and blew up the fortifications of M. Janus, from where the French patrols originated.

Western Front, Winter 1944-45: Alpini of the *Monterosa* Division set in the snow.

Until the coming of spring, activity was only carried out with patrols and counter-attacks, due to the heavy snowfall that prevented other actions. At the beginning of February 1945, it was decided to transfer other units of the "*Monterosa*" to Piedmont to reinforce the defense of the Western Alps, in anticipation of the likely final attack on the part of the French who were bent on revenge for the so-called "*stab in the back*" of 1940 and to seize territory to be used as a bargaining chip in subsequent peace negotiations at the end of the war. Between 6 and 7 February, the 2nd Alpine Regiment, with C.C.R., the 102nd Anti-Tank Company and the Light Column, and the "*Morbegno*" Battalion, were transferred to the Western Alps, defending the valleys of Viù, Ala and Val Grande, with the Command to Lanzo (Torino).

Western Front, Winter 1944-45: a patrol of '*Tirano*' starts for an operation.

Winter 1944-45: Alpini of the *Monterosa*.

In March, it was joined by the "*Brescia*" Battalion that was deployed in the Locana Valley to the right of the "*Morbegno*". With the arrival of "*Brescia*", the regiment extended over a hundred kilometers between the Locana Valley and the Val Chisone, on a defensive line where German units were also located at an altitude of over 2000 meters and with positions and observers between 2,500 and 3,000 meters, with high mountain ranges that made connections between the valleys impossible. The "*Morbegno*" Battalion, in the Valli di Lanzo, deployed its companies between the two valleys that stretch from Lanzo: the Val d'Ala, from which the Val Grande, and the Val di Viù emanate, relieving some German units and the paratroopers of the "*Folgore*" Regiment. The "*Morbegno*" deployed its headquarters to Ceres and deployed its companies to the heads of the valleys with advanced posts along the line of the passes: Regiment Usseglio, the 8th Company, the 7th Company in Balme, the 6th Company in Forno Alpi Graie, the 10th Company in Ceres, and the 9th Company to Viu. The 8th Company dispatched a platoon to Malciausia and a detachment to Lago della Rossa, places where hydroelectric plants of strategic importance were present; The 7th Company dispatched a platoon to the border with France at the Rifugio Gastaldi. During that period no offensive action was taken by French troops, apart from a single attempt crossing the border at Lago della Rossa, which was quickly beaten back with losses on both sides.

In mid-March 1945 the "*Brescia*" Battalion completed its transfer to the Canavese, deploying in the Locana and Orco valleys, at Pont Canavese, with the companies located at the Galisia Pass, Ceresole Reale and Locana. The main task of the battalion was to defend the Alps from any French infiltrations mainly through the Galisia pass, which entered the Isère Valley. There was little partisan activity in the rear area.

In March 1945, the "*Aosta*" Battalion, after its 1st Company had come back from the Garfagnana area, was transferred to Piedmont, along on the Western Alps, deploying its companies in defense of Valle Stura, with its headquarters at the Terme di Vinadio and its companies deployed between Mount Ténibres and Collalunga.

In February 1945 the "*Mantova*" horse-drawn artillery group left the Garfagnana front to be transferred to Piedmont, in the Western Alps. From Garfagnana, the group reached Liguria and then Turin, from where they headed for the Val Susa in early February. It remained in the area for a few weeks, and then on March 30, the headquarters, 10th and 11th Batteries headed for Monginevro, where they took up positions. On the 29th of March, in the Aosta Valley, the 12th Battery was sent to La Thuile, in defense of the Piccolo San Bernardo pass, tactically attached to the 4th Alpine Regiment of the "*Littorio*" Division which was responsible for the defense of the sector.

From the second half of March, the units of the "*Monterosa*" Division, between Piedmont and Valle d'Aosta, from the Colle della Maddalena to Piccolo San Bernardo (over 5,000 men), were the following:

- In Valle Stura: "*Aosta*" Battalion and the 3rd Artillery Group "*Vicenza*"
- In Valle Varaita and Valle Maira: the "*Bassano*" Battalion
- At Monginevro (Torino): "*Tirano*" Battalion and two batteries of the 4th Artillery Group "*Mantova*"
- In the Lanzo Valleys (Torino): the Command of the 2nd Alpine Regiment, with the 102nd Company 'cacciatori di carro' and the Light Column, and the "*Morbegno*" Battalion
- In the Locana Valley (Torino): the "*Brescia*" Battalion
- Piccolo San Bernardo: the 12th Battery of 4th Artillery Group "*Mantova*"

Acknowledgments
The author wishes to give a sincere and warm thanks to the "*Monterosa*" Alpine Division, without its priceless contribution, it would not have been possible to write this article in such detail.

Photographic references
ASFMR - Archivio Storico Fotografico Associazione Monterosa

Spanish in the Waffen SS
By Eduardo M. Gil Martínez
Translated by José Antonio Muñoz Molero

Spanish volunteer of the *Division Azul*.

Oberst Garcia Navarro.

Recruitment

After the withdrawal of the more or less "official" intervention of the Spaniards in the war, first with the *Blue Division* (September-October 1943) and later with the Blue Legion (March-April 1944), as a result of the Allied pressures on the Spanish government, there were several hundred of Spanish citizens who remained in the service of the Reich in very diverse units despite the risk of loss of Spanish nationality that existed to collaborate with the German armed forces. This group was made up of ex-divisionaries (people that belonged to the *Blue Division*) and ex-legionaries in large part, united with other men who crossed the Spanish border to join at their own risk to the German armed forces as well as many Spanish civilians that worked inside of the Reich. After the withdrawal and dissolution of the *Blue Legion* the Spanish intervention with the Axis was illegal, which did not avoid so that some volunteers refused to return to Spain and other Spaniards crossed the border to France. Many of them ended up integrated after many ups and downs in units belonging to the *Waffen SS* (like the "*Wallonien*" or "*Nordland*"), others were assigned to the 3rd Mountain Division or to the 357th Infantry Division. In the same way, other Spaniards fought against the partisan guerrilla in Yugoslavia (August 1944) being part of the 8th Company of the 2nd Battalion of the 3rd Regiment of the *Brandenburg* Division, as well as against the partisan guerrilla in Italy. And as an epic climax, within this group of Spaniards that according to different sources reached about 1000 men, during the last months of the war a small Spanish unit will take part in the defensive combats in the capital of the *Reich*. The causes that moved these men to support the German troops were various. Some men directly did not return with the *Blue Legion* to

Spain after being "*invited*" by German officers to remain in the conflict on their side, enlisting in some units of the *Wehrmacht*. To these men began to incorporate more men from Spain where, in the most pro-German circles, a fairly large number of men (mostly ex-combatants of the *Blue Division*), planned to return to German territory to join them at their own risk, because they didn´t consider his intervention against the Soviet enemy completed.

Soldiers of the *Blue Legion*, already with the Spanish uniform, before leaving for Spain.

The general Agustin Muñoz Grandes, welcomes the veterans of the *Blue Division* in Spain.

At the same time and even before the *Blue Legion* was disbanded, in circles close to the Falange, the formation of a new unit of Spanish troops at the service of the Germans begins. The recruitment had to be secret, to avoid the intention of Francisco Franco, to stop all these activities. Other "*volunteers*" come from unemployed or Spanish workers in the *Reich*, as well as some Spanish exiles (former Republicans) who after having served in work battalions have been forced to wear the German uniform sometimes. But the Spanish authorities will not make it easy, for which the border crossings of the Pyrenees were "*shielded*" in direct contact with occupied France. The civil guard (guardia civil) was given strict orders to prevent these men from crossing, with the order to shoot them if necessary. Although many of them who attempted to cross the border were shot or killed under the border guard fire, others did manage to get to France.

Summer 1944: spanish volunteers of the *Freiwilligen Einheit Stablack*, with *Wehrmacht* uniforms, in Romania (*C.C.Jurado*).

Luis Garcia Valdajos.

Spanish volunteers in Germany, 1944.

To better organize the newcomers, the Germans established recruiting stations, where these men would be documented and integrated into the German Armed Forces through the *Sonderstab F*. The recruitment units belonging to Dr. Edwin Maxel's *Sonderstab F* operated from January 1944 to August of the same year in southern France, with "offices" in the border regions near Andorra, Port Bou, Hendaye, Puigcerdá and its main headquarters located in the city of Lourdes. Once registered at the headquarters of *Sonderstab F*, the new recruits were sent to a receiving camp in the Quartier de la Reine in Versailles. There they were received by Luis García Valdajos, a veteran of the Blue Division and Blue Legion who was in Versailles, destined from the training center of Stablack Süd (in East Prussia), with the mission of coordinating and escorting the contingents of Spaniards to Stablack. After being submitted to the corresponding medical check-up, almost all the admitted ones were transferred to Stablack, whereas a few were recruited by the SD for a new unit created in February of 1944, the

Einsatzgruppe Pyrenären of the *Sonderstab F,* destined in antipartisans tasks through its infiltration in the Resistance. At the end of April or beginning of May of 1944 *Spanisches-Freiwilligen-Einheit* was created in Stablack, with initial troops near 250 men.

Winter 1943-1944: *Waffen SS* **Spanish volunteers at Sennheim camp. The volunteer at the center, carries the badge of the** *Falange.* **The other two, are veterans of the** *Blue Division* **(U.S. NARA).**

Spanish volunteers on the *Signal.*

At least since June 1944, a group of Spaniards were quickly put into action serving in the *Sicherheitsdienst* (SD). Their missions were realized mainly in southwest France including information tasks although they also participated in actions against the French resistance and against the allies in Normandy.

Since dates as early as May of 1944, the Spanish Government knows the existence of Spaniards enlisted in the *Waffen SS* as shown by the two letters sent from the Embassy of Spain in Berlin to the Ministry of Foreign Affairs of Spain dealing with this subject are. On May 11, 1944, the Spanish consul in Berlin sent the following letter to the Spanish foreign minister: "*It has been reported that the border of the Pyrenees is now being smuggled by many ex-combatants of the Blue Division, with the assurance that they will be welcomed by the German authorities ... several of these ex-combatants have hastened to enlist in the Flemish Legion of the SS to re-fight the Russian front* ". In a letter dated 6 July 1944, the Spanish ambassador in Berlin reported to the Spanish Foreign Minister on the clandestine presence of Spaniards in the German armed forces, the following could be read: "*Many of these Spaniards display national emblems in their uniforms (refers to Spanish emblems) apart from the distinctive SS ...* ".

Spanish volunteers at Stockerau, 1944.

So the Spanish embassy in Berlin estimated that by the summer of 1944, there were about 1500 Spaniards working for the German security services in French territory; although possibly this figure was increased. The first group of Spaniards under the command of García Valdajos had to arrive in Stablack on April 15 where they underwent an endless training, although many of them had previously been combatants. The number of Spaniards welcomed in Versailles reached 250-300 by May 1944 and a figure close to 400 in June, where after the corresponding classification were sent to East Prussia to be enlisted in the *Freiwilligen Einheit Stablack* under the command of the Artillery Captain Gräfe and the second lieutenants Loinant and Panther. Once the Spaniards had settled there, García Valdajos was acquiring an administrative control role in the training of the new recruits until June (day 6), leaving the purely military tasks to be carried out by Ezquerra. An important fact to keep in mind is that it was decided that the Spanish soldiers would wear the *Wehrmacht* uniform.

An armed guard of Todt organization.

At the beginning of June 1944, the 400-man unit moved from Stablack to the towns of Stockerau and Hollabrun, near Vienna, where it would be called the *Freiwilligen Einheit Stockerau*. Their first two companies, already completed, marched to the town of Solbad Hall im Tirol (now Hall im Tirol), near Innsbruck, to receive training as mountain troops for eight weeks. The entire unit will be named *Freiwilligen Einheit Solbad Hall* and its two companies, *101st Spanische-Freiwilligen Kompanie*

and *102nd Spanische-Freiwilligen Kompanie*. From this group of men, about 50 were transferred to the Todt organization in the South of France for several reasons.

In the Karstjäger

After the training was completed in August 1944, the soldiers will be fitted into German units as diverse as the 357th Infantry Division, the 3rd Gebirgs Division or the Anti-Partisan units of the 3rd Regiment of the Brandenburg Division. Another contingent of Spaniards served for the SD and about 50 men performed antipartisan tasks in the area of the Pyrenees until being transferred to the Jadgverbande of Otto Skorzeny. The 101st, company attached to the *3.Gebirgs-Division* (belonging to the *XVII.Armee-Korps* of the Group of armies South Ukraine of the *Wehrmacht*), departed from Solbad im Hall Tirol by train until Vienna from where they will set off to the Bucovina where they will arrive in the middle of August of 1944.

Soldiers of the *Brandenburg* Division during an anti-partisan operation in Jugoslavia, 1944.

A *Karstjäger* unit before an anti-partisan operation.

Possibly a number of men who totaled a company (the 102nd), were entrusted to carry out anti-partisan fighting in Yugoslavia, in present-day Slovenia. The Spaniards commanded by Lieutenant Ortiz appear to have been integrated into the 8th Company of the 2nd Battalion of the 3rd Regiment of the *Brandenburg* Division. Part of these men remained in the north of Yugoslavia with order to fight to Tito's partisans; another group that extended its antipartisans tasks towards Italian territory led by the lieutenants Ortiz and Demetrio following the 7th Company with which they will face the Italian partisan troops in localities such as Bevagna, Perugia, Arsoli, Carsoli, Avezzano or Terni, and later met with other "*Brandenburgers*" north of Turin in September 1944 (specifically in Ivrea), from where they will retreat to the south of France, although some of the Spaniards were leave behind and incorporated into the "*Karstjäger*".

Summer 1944: *Karstjäger* during operation *Annemarie*, conducted along the borders of the *Reich* and in the province of Ljubljana.

A *Karstjäger* soldier on the cover of the magazine 'Adria Illustrierte', April 1945.

At the end of October, as a result of the advance of the Soviet army and the Tito's Yugoslav forces, there were withdrawals of the German troops, causing some of the Spaniards who had deployed through northern Italy were left behind, being absorbed by the *SS-Gebirgsjäger-Regiment 59* of the *24.Waffen-Gebirgs-Division der SS "Karstjäger"*, under the command of the *Sturmbannführer* Werner Hahn. Here they would concentrate on a Spanish company with denomination *5.Kmp./II.Btl.* (*Spanish-Kmp.*) belonging to the *SS-Gebirs-Regiment 59*, under the command of *W-Ustuf.* Ortiz Fernández. According to Ortiz's testimony, he held a course in Solbad Hall im Tirol to qualify as an officer of the *Waffen-SS*, after which he recruited Spaniards through factories and prison camps around Vienna. With these men would increase the potential of his 5th Company of the 2nd Battalion, which he would command with the rank of *Untersturmführer*. The *Karstjäger* fought from November 1944 mainly in the region of Friuli-Venezia Giulia (in German Julisch Venetien) to northeast Italy, west of Slovenia and Croatia with remarkable success. The Spanish Company would be fully operational with an approximate number of about 100 men between November and December, acting in antipartisan tasks in Villach and Pontebba, and later in Tolmezzo. In March of 1945 they acted in the area of Trieste in the battle that took place in the city of Gorizia against Tito's partisans troops. According to the testimony of a "*Karstjäger*" German veteran, the Spanish company was very aggressive in the combats that were developed mainly in the sector of Chiaporano, in which the combat ended up being body to body. On April 8, the section commanded by the *Oberscharführer* Trápaga, was surrounded in Ponte di Canale, suffering major casualties. The combats against Yugoslav and Italian partisans caused a multitude of atrocities on both sides. The men of the "*Karstjäger*" at the end of the war also fought in the regions occupied by the English troops arriving to confront the famous British Desert Rats.

SS-Ostubaf. Skorzeny in the Schwedt area, February 1945.

Leutnant Helmut Demetrio, at right in the photo, with some members of his unit.

Spanish with Skorzeny

About the Spaniards enlisted in the Brandenburg (now withdrawing to France), were integrated in *8.Kompanie II.Bataillon 3.Regiment* "BR" belonging to the "*Streifkorps Biscaya*" as part of the "*Streifkorps Süd-Frankreich*". To these men commanded by Lieutenant Helmut Demetrio would join some Spaniards coming from the organization Todt constituting the denominated *Einsatzgruppe Pyrenären* from July 1944, that fought the maquis in the south and the south-east of France; totaling about 50 men. The *Einsatzgruppe Pyrenären* during his period of activity was distinguished in the antipartisan fight against the maquis, but they had to withdraw from France during the summer of 1944 along with *Streifkorps Süd-Frankreich* before the advance of the allied forces. In September 1944, when the *Abwehr* was absorbed, the *Streifkorps Süd-Frankreich* was transferred to the *SS-Jagdverväng Südwest* under the command of the *Obersturmbannführer* Otto Skorzeny. Possibly the men of Demetrio attached to the *Einsatzgruppe Pyrenären* that would be around 20-30 men, constituted the denominated "*Kommando Kondor*", attached to the *SS-Jagdeinsatz Süd-Frankreich*. They were destined in a base close to Molsheim (an Alsatian town), to combat the infiltrations of French collaborators in the liberated regions. From January 1945, the Spaniards of the "*Kommando Kondor*" joined the reconnaissance and sabotage missions in the rear of the US 7th Army. In April 1945, the *SS-Jagdvervänd Südwest* merged into the *SS-Jagdvervänd Mitte*; at that time the latter was personally commanded by Skorzeny.

Spanish volunteers belonging to the *Wallonien*.

With the Walloons of Degrelle and the 29th SS-Division

From October 1944, the remains of the Spanish units that fought in Yugoslavia (102nd) are grouped in Stockerau and Hollabrunn with those who fought in the Carpathians (101st) and with the 3rd Company that had finished training with the volunteers who had kept coming. At this time, the *Spanisches-Freiwilligen-Einheit* was incorporated into the Croatian Depot Brigade (*Kroatisches-Ersatz-Brigade*). The situation of "waiting" of the Spanish troops stationed in Stockerau, allowed that already from the early date of the 11 to 17 of December 1944, 33 men left the Austrian quartering with destination to the *28.SS-Freiw.Pz.Gren.Div. "Wallonien"*.

Wallonien officers at *SS-Panzergrenadier-Schule* of Kienschlag. At center, With right arm on his hip, *SS-Ustuf*. Roger de Goy. To his left, the *Sturmscharführer* Lorenzo Ocañas.

On January 25, 1945, the Military District XVII (Vienna) established the 101st and 102nd Spanish Voluntary Companies as reinforcements of the 357th Infantry Division that would be deployed east of Bratislava. This would have been the fate of the remains of both companies, although everything changed due to the "escape" at the beginning of February 1945 from some of these men to the *28.SS-Freiwilligen-Panzergrenadier-Division "Wallonien"* following his formerly escaped companions thanks to the mediation of Van Horembeke (Belgian nationalized Spanish), to the town of Hemmendorf where the location of the *Wallonien* Depot was at that time. Among these first Spaniards attracted for the *"Wallonien"* were several non-commissioned officers with considerable experience in combat with both the *Blue Division* and the *Blue Legion* on the Eastern Front (such as Zabala, Ocañas, Cabrera or Pinar). As a first step, these men were allowed to recover their old ranks, lost until that time.

A group of young volunteers for the *Wallonien*, during the training in the Summer of 1943.

Ricardo Botet Moro.

Taking advantage of the presence of these Spaniards, it was traced everywhere the existence of Spaniards who could join to the *"Wallonien"*. It is difficult to say with accuracy the number of men who joined the Belgians from both camps, but it was possible that between them and those recruited in other areas could be formed almost independent unit and commanded exclusively by Spaniards and commanded by García Valdajos. At the end of November 1944 the first contingent of Spanish volunteers was concentrated in the camp that the Walloon division had in Breslau. The final number of Spaniards that were enlisted in the *"Wallonien"* could ascend to more than one hundred according to some sources, although more possibly was reached to the 240-350 men in January of 1945 that were integrated in the unique battalion of the 70 Regiment of infantry SS of the division to whose command was the *SS-Hstuf*. Denie, giving rise to the formation of a third company in the same (the 3/I/70). Wallons and Spanish troops left Breslau and were stationed first in Olderhof (near Hannover) and were subsequently sent to the Rhineland area, where they were prepared for a possible intervention in the offensive of the Bulge (Ardennes), in which they did not finally take part, although on 24 December 1944 a group of Spaniards under the command of *SS-Oscha*. Botet was in the area of Marmagen (Nettersheim) integrated into the *SS-Ostuf*. Derriks' group. Once left the western front, they will go in February to Stettin (now Szczecin) and Stargard sector (currently Stargard Szczeciński). Even in the final stages of the training and before combats, another "transfer" of men from one unit to another occurred, so that a group of about 30 Italian volunteers got permission to join the *29.Waffen Grenadier Division der SS "(Italienische Nr 1)"*.

Waffen-Oberscharführer der SS **Giorgio Gandini on the right, with the Spanish** *Waf.-Oscha. der SS* **Camargo, during military maneuvers by the Italian SS Training Battalion (I./WGRdSS 81), in March 1945, near Rodengo-Saiano (*Corbatti-Nava Collection*).**

Together with the Italians, about ten or twenty Spaniards should be added, who may have preferred to move to another area of the conflict closest to Spain, and this small group of Spaniards was under *SS-Oscha*. Camargo and *SS-Uscha*. Martínez Alberich, who will be integrated into the Italian division directing a section of SS-Regiment 81 belonging to the *29.Waffen Grenadier Division of SS "(Italienische Nr 1)"* mainly dedicated to antipartisan tasks, arriving only at the end of the conflict to face American troops with acceptable results given the circumstances in the last days of the conflict in Europe and possibly taking part in combats close to Trieste and Brenner. Since mid-January 1945, the hitherto relatively inactive Soviets, carry out a strong offensive that breaks the Front of the Vistula.

Léon Degrelle on the Pomeranian front.

SS Grenadier on the Pomeranian front.

Wallonien grenadiers in combat, 1945.

Only in a few weeks they reach the river Oder, which led the German forces to retreat and redo their defenses again. In order to establish a secure defensive front, new troops are claimed to the front line on the Eastern Front; among them is the Walloon unit (magnificently studied by Norling). On January 27, the *"Wallonien"*, along with the Belgian too (but Flemish not Wallons) *27.SS-Freiwilligen-Grenadier-Division "Langemarck"*, are ordered to go to Stargard, where they arrive on 6 February. Already in their area of deployment, the Spaniards received new compatriots who were integrated into their unit. The zone entrusted to the Walloons for the defense, is located to the south of the city of Stargard, being like force of reserve the unique Battalion of the 2º Regiment that is where they integrated the Spaniards conforming its 3rd Company.

On the 11th, in the context of the battle for Arnswalde, the 1st Company of the 1st Battalion of the *SS-Freiwilligen-Grenadier-Regiment 69* (among which some Spaniards), temporarily assigned to the *SS-Panzer-Division 'Frundsberg'*, tries to conquer the village of Klutzow although the final result is the defeat with the subsequent retreat. On February 16, 1945, Operation *"Sonnenwende"* (Solstice) commenced, including the divisions SS *"Frundsberg"*, *"Nordland"*, *"Langemarck"*, *"SS-Polizei"*, *"Nederland"* and *"Wallonien"* All under the joint command of the *SS-Obergruppenführer* Felix Steiner. The subsequent reorganization of the forces still "standing" in that sector, leads the *"Wallonien"* to be subordinated under the control of the most powerful *"Nordland"*. On February 27, the Soviets moved forward with the intention of sieging the troops at Stargard; starting the Battle for Stargard. The casualties are numerous again, so that the only *SS-Freiwilligen-Grenadier-Regiment 70* (also called 3/I/70) Battalion, where the Spaniards were placed, has to be dissolved and its troops divided in the two Battalions of the *SS-Freiwilligen-Grenadier-Regiment 69*. Here the Spaniards, joined forces with the Walloons, will destroy the Soviet tanks, mainly the well-known *T-34*, with their new anti-tank weapons (the dreaded panzerfaust), stopping as much as possible the Soviet advance. On March 3, the remains of the disappeared 1st Battalion of the 70th SS Infantry Regiment of the division cover the retreat of the "*Wallonien*" along the Baltic coast. On March 4, Stargard is definitely abandoned, with only about 60 Spaniards who managed to escape the siege in early March 1945.

German Grenadiers in Stargard, February 1945.

German defensive position.

Grenadiers and *Panzer* during an attack, March 1945.

The Stargard survivors will be regrouped in Scheune, south of Stettin, where they were initially part of a line Defense north of Berlin. They were there for little time, since immediately they received orders so that all the Spaniards that were in the Walloon division, were to concentrate in the environs of Potsdam, fact that took place towards the first days of March taking advantage that the units of III Germanic Corps of the SS retired towards the capital of the Reich too.

These men will be part of the Ezquerra Unit made up of at least two companies of men, who were nominally adhered to the "*Nordland*" in the defense of Berlin; although this story requires a separate chapter. Possibly some of the Spaniards of the *Wallonien* did not retreat to Potsdam and continue until the end of the conflict with the Walloon Unit, scattered among their companies as Degrelle himself made known in an interview.

With the Bozen and the Dirlewanger.

There are also reports of the existence of a few Spanish men in another unit under the double rune such as *SS-Polizei Freiwilligen Bataillon Bozen*, where it is said that they came to form between 20-31 Spanish. The origin of the Spanish in this unit is unclear, and may well have been from the *24.Waffen Gebirgs Division "Karstjäger"*. Since the *I.Btl./SS-Pol.Rgt. "Bozen"* coincided at the end of April 1945 in the same area of deployment as the "*Karstjäger*", the Tarvisio area. Of the approximately 100 men who would be in the mountain unit, about 20 or 31 may have been authorized to join in the *SS-Polizei Freiwilligen Bataillon Bozen*, being arranged in Italy until the end of the war in the fight against the partisans.

An unit of *SS-Polizei Freiwilligen Bataillon Bozen* during an anti-partisan operation (*KB Trainotti*)

Finally, another unit in which documents refer to the presence of Spaniards is the *SS-Sonder Bataillon "Dirlewanger"*, where the name of 6 Spaniards in their 1st Company appears. With this unit incorporated in the *SS-Kampfgruppe Anhalt* took part in Operation *"Frühlingfest"* in Belarus. Little more is known of the Spaniards of this Unit of penitentiary origin, although they are supposed to continue in it until the end of the conflict, being able to participate in the atrocious repression of the rise of Warsaw.

Warsaw 1944: German soldiers engaged in fighting to repress the uprising against Polish insurgents.

Some other Spaniards served in other German units very possibly in a punctual way, as in the *Kriegsmarine* (Naval Deposit 28 in Sennheim), in naval coast artillery units in Estonia, the Organization *Todt*, the NSKK, the Legion *"Speer"* or even in an artillery regiment from *17.Luftwaffen-Felddivision* during the summer of 1944 in the Norman coast.

Bibliography

"Bajo las banderas del III Reich alemán. Españoles en Rusia, 1941-1945", Defensa. Mayo 1999.

Wayne H. Bowen, *"The Ghost Battalion: Spaniards in the Waffen-SS, 1944-1945"*, The Historian, vol. 63.

Carlos Caballero Jurado, *"El batallón fantasma. Españoles en la Wehrmacht y Waffen-SS, 1944-45"*, CEHRE y ACTV, Alicante-Valencia, 1987.

Eduardo M. Gil Martínez, *"Españoles en las SS y la Wehrmacht 1944-45. La Unidad Ezquerra en la batalla de Berlín"*, Editorial Almena. 2011.

Eduardo M. Gil Martínez, *"The spanish in the SS and Wehrmacht 1944-45. The Ezquerra unit in the battle of Berlin"*, Schiffer Military History. 2012.

G. Tambs, L. Kleinfeld, *"La división española de Hitler. La División Azul en Rusia"*, Editorial San Martín.

Sven Erik Norling, *"Guerreros de Borgoña. Historia de los voluntarios valones de León Degrelle en el Frente del Este. El ocaso de los Dioses (1944-1945)"*, García Hispán Editor. 2008.

J.P. Sourd, *"True Believers. Spanish Volunteers in the Heer and Waffen-SS, 1944-1945"*, Europa Books.

Jean-Pierre Sourd, *"Croisés d´un idéal"*, Dualpha. 2007.

Gregorio Torres Gallego, *"Españoles en las Waffen SS. Italia, 1945"*, Revista Española de Historia Militar, nº10. 2001.

German perception of volunteers of the Muslim division of the SS
by Dmitry Frolov

SS-Brigadeführer **Karl Sauberzweig. As an experienced commander Sauberzweig understood importance of providing close connection between Islam and National Socialism within his division (NARA).**

Military service of Bosnians in SS-troop formations (*Waffen SS*) marked the new stage of recruiting Muslims to the German army from the beginning of the war against the USSR. The division, which was supposed to be actively used at the place of its formation (Bosnia and Herzegovina), needed very intense support from Islamic politicians and the German command, which emphasized the importance of Bosnians' efforts in establishing the *"New Order"* in the Balkans. *SS-Brigadeführer* and Major General of the *Waffen SS* Karl-Gustav Sauberzweig as the division commander aimed at creating a single combat group, united just like other *Waffen SS* units. Relations between different categories of military servicemen within the division became a vital question in the context of effectiveness of its future combat use. Thus, as expected, national-religious preferences of the SS newcomers became a major obstacle to accomplishing the objective as stated by the division commander. The reason for such sharp contradictions was the fact that so called *"political soldiers"* appeared in the *Waffen SS* structure – these people didn't have a lot to do with these elite units of the Nazi state. Racial doctrine, an essential part of the Third Reich, became one of the first problems for creating a combat unit, unified by the idea of fellowship, widely spread across the *Waffen SS*. But the cultural gap between the German SS-soldiers, who had previous military service in elite divisions, and Bosnian ex-farmers and workmen turned out to be a problem for attempts to combine religious and Nazi ideas in the new formation. With reference to this there is the example of a German SS-officer, transferred to the Muslim SS-division from the *"Das Reich"* SS armored division. He was unsatisfied with his service in the "legionary division", which, to his mind, was of much lower status than his previous duty assignment. Heinrich

Himmler's idea to use the experience of the Hapsburg monarchy and create their own elite Bosnian military units didn't fit the frame of the Nazi state, either.

The Grand Mufti of Jerusalem was a spiritual advisor of the division and contributed to close interrelation of the Third Reich with Islamic world (NARA).

The Nuremberg race laws, adopted in 1935, formed the basis of creating the "super-human" complex in German society, together with disregard of representatives of other nations. Failures, which followed the German army from the middle of the war, and the war itself, forced Nazi apologists to look for more reasons to involve foreigners into first the Wehrmacht and then the Waffen SS. For cases of recruiting Balkan Muslims into the Waffen SS, the latter had to establish trustworthy relations between Muslims and Germans, based on necessity of co-existence of National-Socialist and Islamic ideas within the division. Sauberzweig mentioned that the Bosnians willingly adopted the ideas of National-Socialist theory, receiving them via their commanders. As for unit commanders Sauberzweig had an opinion, different from *SS-Obergruppenführer* A. Phleps', who claimed it was necessary for Bosnians not to focus on their commanders' personalities, but to accept them as ambassadors of the Führer's will. The division commander believed that Muslims, as the "*Balkan primitive people*" representatives were fully focused on personalities of their commanders, whose manner of behavior was copied by their Muslim subordinates. "*He will give his fidelity to the officer, who wins his heart, like a child. He has a deeply developed feeling of justice and honor*" – stated Sauberzweig. As another problem he stated the necessity to save the basis of Islam among the German regular personnel and together with it to save understanding of the importance of subordinate soldiers' religious needs. In this regard a lot depended on division "spiritual guides" – imams, who had to both organize religious ceremonies and increase the level of empathy and understanding among German soldiers.

Ethnic German *SS-Uscha.* Zvonimir Bernwald. Within the division he conducted military service in VI squadron – unit, responsible for spirit and belief work with personnel assets.

SS-Gruppenführer Artur Phleps in a Moroccan-style tarboosh. This type of tarboosh would become the main headwear of Muslim SS-division.

Sauberzweig was one of the few who put much effort into making German officers understand the importance of the imams institution.

To do that the battalion officers asked German SS-officers to visit the mosque in Brcko, where the latter presented a short report on cultural and religious topics, referring to traditions and rules, developed in the territory of Bosnia. When characterizing subordinates the division commander first of all emphasized the necessity of understanding Muslims. According to his report to *SS-Obergruppenführer* G.Berger, *SS-Obersturmführer* Geze *"didn't understand either the Muslim temper or their logic"* due to his Westphalian background, and *SS-Hauptsturmführer* E.Wangemann, who was transferred to the division by *SS-Reichsführer "could hardly understand the existing situation and had strained relations with his colleagues, commanders and imams"*. Muslims had poor relations with ethnic Germans as well. This was not limited to reference to the Volksdeutsche of SS-Division *"Prinz Eugen"*, responsible for mass murders in Košutica. When transferred to the Muslim SS-Division, they despised Bosnians and considered them to be *"subhuman"*. As stated by the report of a German people's unit führer in Croatia, families of German SS-soldiers reacted quite negatively to the news of recruiting Muslims into the *Waffen SS*. Local German citizens considered Bosnians "imperfect", too (relying on experience of working with refugees and conflicts with smugglers). It became unclear how Muslims got into the Waffen SS, since it caused the collapse of all the previous propaganda work, due to which only the Germanic peoples could serve in the Waffen SS. This equalization of ethnic Germans' rights with foreign volunteers caused puzzlement and loss of pride of doing military service in the *Waffen SS*. But the *SS-Reichsführer*, who enjoyed the idea of active use of Muslim volunteers' potential by the *Waffen SS*, was not overly concerned with that matter. By his opinion, equal rights lead to establishing fellowship between all categories of military personnel: *"There's no difference between Reichdeutsche, Bosnians, Croatians or South-Eastern Germans for creating the spirit of fellowship. We wear the same uniform, fix our belts with the same buckle and have the same badges"*. Himmler considered it important to meet all religious preferences of the volunteers. Thus he supported the division commander. The "Special unbreakable right" of all Muslims - members of the Waffen SS and police – meant they could avoid pork and alcohol in food. This was seen from the perspective of promoting the stability of the Muslim soldiers.

German officers show the important guest combat skills of their subordinates. Neuhammer shooting range. Silesia, 1943.

The Grand Mufti of Jerusalem al-Husseini greeting the soldiers of SS Muslim division. Neuhammer shooting range. Silesia, November, 1943

The *SS-Reichsführer* ordered all officers, squadron commanders and heads of supply corps to bear that in mind when organizing provision and food. *"We mustn't reject thousands of fanatic Muslim volunteers and their families because of narrow mindedness and stubbornness of certain people"* – Himmler said. What's interesting here, is that at first German the command couldn't organize food supplies for the division in France.

Training of the *Handschar* Division at Neuhammer Training Grounds in Autumn of 1943.

As *SS-Hauptsturmführer* E. Romberg said, this lead to reduction of a "common attitude" among Muslim soldiers. Meanwhile SS-soldiers were forced to do the hardest work with public disciplinary punishments for the smallest mistakes. To solve that problem division commander Sauberzweig sent the *SS-Reichsführer* a letter with a request to increase the food allowance of the division. By emphasizing enthusiasm, obedience and loyalty of Muslim soldiers Sauberzweig managed to get a positive response from Hitler. Supplies, including better food allowance, were supposed to be the most efficient tool for improving the state of morale of soldiers by establishing a relationship of trus between them and the Germans. What led to tense relations between Catholic Croatians and Muslims was propaganda work, devoted to Muslims, and the Bosnian status of the division, marked by its name. One hundred twenty-one Catholic Croatians deserted from the division while it was in France. This was mainly caused by Croatians rejecting the idea of autonomy of the Independent State of Croatia together with disappointment in service with the division. Except for specific peculiarities the Muslim SS-division had problems not connected to the Islamic character of the unit. Difficulties in cooperation between Germans and Bosnians were expected, but racial prejudice affected two other categories of the division's servicemen – Reichs and Volksdeutsche. *SS-Hauptsturmführer* Romberg noticed the unwillingness of Reichsdeutsche commanders to study the volunteers' language together with zero tolerance to Volksdeutsche conversations in Croatian. Their, as they believed, higher Reichdeutsche status was emphasized by refusal to live in the same room with Volksdeutsche, who were forced to live with their soldiers. We must state that German command did their best to solve all the problems, despite the obvious issues which affected the first "non-Germanic" division of the *Waffen SS*.

Handschar soldiers, Autumn 1943.

Grand Mufti and Handschar soldiers.

The *SS-Reichsführer* published an order, forbidding the ignoring of cultural and religious peculiarities of Bosnian SS-soldiers, since he understood it was unacceptable to limit religious rights and freedoms of Muslim soldiers. Stubbornness on the part of certain people who not willing to follow the rules necessary for the division caused Himmler to call it *"stubborn commissionerism"*. He issued orders to prevent it in the harshest possible way, without paying attention to ranks and duty positions of the guilty. As for the problem of establishing understanding between Germans and Muslim soldiers we should agree with the opinion of German historian Stefan Petke. He has stated a fair doubt regarding the possibility of creating a unit, unified by common weaponry, instructions or badges only. Sauberzweig, an experienced officer who knew the true meaning of *"trench brotherhood"*, understood that, also. A commander must not miss any single opportunity to influence their subordinates. The fighting cohesiveness, capable of overcoming any crisis or combat-tension, was created during talks at rest breaks, route marches, rest points or *"with an evening cigarette"*, when soldiers shared their cares or asked for advice. But reality did not meet the attempts of certain commanders and of the division commander to influence the situation. The dominating Nazi racial doctrine of *"alien elements"* completely neutralized the Germans' experience in creating such units. This happened despite the re-thinking of relations between German and Muslim SS-soldiers, which happened nearly at the end of war, even for purposes of propaganda.

Bibliography

National Archives and Records Administration (NARA T175 R70).

Lappin E., *"Rolle der Waffen-SS beim zwangsarbeitseinsatz ungarischer juden im gau Steiermark und bei den todesmarschen ins kz Mauthausen"*.

Центральный архив Министерства обороны Российской Федерации. Ф. 500. (Central Archive of the Ministry of Defense of the Russian Federation. F. 500).

Petke S., *"Militärische Vergemeinschaftung Versuche muslimischer Soldaten in der Waffen-SS. Die Beispiele der Division «Handschar» und des «Osttürkischen Waffenverbands der SS»"*

Kazimirović V., *"NDH u svetlu nemećkih dokumenata i dnevnika Gleza fon Horstenau. 1941-1945"*

Sulejmanpasic Z., *"13. SS Divizija «Handzar». Istine i lazi"*.

Lepre G., *"Himmler's Bosnian division. The Waffen-SS Handschar Division 1943-1945"*

Zaugg F. A., *"Albanische Muslime in der Waffen-SS. Von «Grossalbanien» zur Division «Scanderbeg»"*

A Swedish Hero: Gösta Hallberg-Cuula
by Erik Norling

Hallberg-Cuula on the cover of the most distributed non political Swedish magazine, March 1940.

A Finnish machine gun crew during the Winter War.

Between 1939-1945, the small country of Finland, with a population of not even 3.7 million, was involved in three wars: The Winter War (1939-1940), the Continuation War (1941-1944) and the Lapponian War (1944-1945). The first one standing alone against Stalin's aggression; the second one to recover the lost territories and secure the border against the dangerous neighbour and the third one a short and relatively bloodless campaign to expel the withdrawing German troops still in Finland after the armistice with the Soviet Union September 1944. It has been calculated that around 12.000 Swedish volunteers fought in the Finnish Army during the Winter and Continuation War. This was a high percentage considering that Sweden had then a population of only around 6,5 million. These wars created many legends and heroes, many controversial due to their political engagement. The most famous was to be Lauri Törni, one of the most decorated Finnish soldiers, an officer in the *Waffen-SS* and later KIA in Vietnam as US Colonel in the Special Forces. His life was depicted in John Wayne's movie *Green Berets* (1968). Not to be forgotten also was Georg von Haartman, Colonel in General Franco's army during the Spanish Civil War or the Swedish Major Martin Ekström who fought not one but five wars against the Bolsheviks between 1917-1944. However, the most known Swedish legend to be was Gösta Hallberg-Cuula.

Sven Olof Lindholm, leader of the Swedish Nationalsocialist party.

Gösta Hallberg-Cuula during the Winter War, 1940, with the "Death Patrull´s sign at the helmet.

Youth and political engagement

Gösta (but registered as Gustaf when enlisted) Eugén Hallberg-Cuula was born in the Swedish capital, Stockholm, the 4th November 1912 in a Swedish-speaking family from Finland that had emigrated to Sweden decades before. He received his baptism in the Finnish Lutheran Church of the Swedish capital. His father, Captain Carl Hallberg-Cuula, died when he was only two years old leaving his mother Fanny alone. He became a philosophy student at the University of Stockholm, served his military service as volunteer between 1931-1932, first as Corporal and ending as Sergeant of the Swedish Army in the Reserve. Soon after he would became politically active[1]. With strong anticommunist feelings he engaged in political activities of the several existing Swedish National Socialist parties. He joined not even being 18 years old the NSAP (Swedish Workers National Socialist Party), led by Sven Olof Lindholm, receiving the member number 240 and assumed despite his youth the rank of Propaganda Chief of this small party of Stockholm's branch. He was the founder of the Youth Organisation (*Nordik Ungdom* – Nordic Youth) between 1932-1933. In 1939, the party changed their name to SSS (*Swedish Socialist Union*) but remained loyal to their National Socialist program and Gösta Hallberg-Cuula soon began to be considered one of the most active members. Every year his greetings to the party and his name was reproduced in the special number for the Christmas magazine *Den Svenske Nationalsocialisten* (The Swedish National Socialist)[2].

The first volunteer to enlist

When the Soviet Union assaulted Finland in the autumn 1939, Hallberg-Cuula joined as volunteer in the Finnish Army. He was unmarried and became the first party member to do so. Many others would follow him and were KIA during WW2. He served during the

in World War Two 1939-1945

Winter War in a Swedish-speaking unit (the Second Company 2./JR10) as Sergeant since the 5th December 1939. He commanded a so called *dödspatrull* (Suicide patrol) of six men that infiltrated enemy lines. On one occasion his unit killed 43 Russian soldiers and was awarded the 12th January 1940 the *Frihets medaljen* Second Class (Liberty medal – Fm II).

The NCO Hallberg-Cuula during the Winter War.

At the Hangö front, Autumn 1941 with his International Platoon.

A few days later, the 10th February, he lost at the bloody Summa Front his left eye, after being wounded by a bullet in the head at Marjonpellomäki, and since then he wore the patch that made in legendary. Wounded and ending the Winter War he was promoted to *Fänrik* (Aspirant Officer) due to his courage receiving the Finnish *Frihetskorset* (Liberty Cross – Frk IV) of 4th Class and the *Frihets medaljen* First Class (Fm I). The Swedish magazine *SE,* one of the most widely sold magazines in the country, dedicated him the cover of the special number and a photographic reportage inside where the Swedish flag on his chest is seen clearly[3].

The Continuation War

In June 1941 Operation Barbarossa was launched, and the Finnish armies joined the Third Reich. Immediately Swedish volunteers enlisted massively and in Summer 1941 the Swedish Volunteer Bataillon with the first 800 volunteers incorporated into the Swedish speaking regiment JR55 was deployed at the Hangö front, besieging a Russian naval base west of Helsinki. Hallberg-Cuula, enlisted the 29th June still being under rehabilitation for his heavy wounds from the Winter War and travelled to Finland early July 1941. He received the command of the so called "International Platoon" in the Volunteer Bataillon. This Platoon integrated volunteers of at least 12 nationalities, including even a Spaniard (Sergeant Del Prado) as well as Germans, Hungarians, Norwegians, Danes, etc.[4]. Being at Hangö, a group of party members, led by the Sergeant Otto Hallberg (not to be confused with Hallberg-Cuula, not being relatives) decided in August to organize a party section at the front to keep contact with the home front. The first meeting was held at the front the 28th August and Hallberg-Cuula held a speech for the party members that attended. They named it "*Sveaborg*", the Swedish fort at the entrance of Helsinki that had protected the capital from the Russian invaders over the centuries[5]. In November 1941, the Russians left Hangö and the Bataillon was disbanded in December. Soon a new volunteer unit was organized named the Swedish Volunteer Company that was attached to the Swedish speaking regiment JR13 that served in the Finnish Army at the Svirfront, close to Lake Ladoga.

Gösta Hallberg-Cuula, Winter 1942.

Around 400 volunteers would serve in this unit between 1942-1944[6], a high percentage being members of the several Swedish National Socialist or Fascist parties. Now as Reserve Lieutenant, wearing proudly now his newly given *Frihetskorset* (Liberty Cross – Frk III) of 3rd Class, Hallberg-Cuula was among the first to join the Company and was to lead a Platoon when deployed at the Jandeba river.

The 14th April 1942, Hallberg-Cuula was killed by a landmine. He decided to join his men in the dangerous task of cleaning a mined area to enable them to have a route to send patrols into enemy territory. He was trying to deactivate one when it was activated and he died almost immediately. His Battalion CO, Major Sven Hedengren, also a party member, wrote into the Battalion daily report "*Today was KIA the brave, veteran of the Winter War, Hallberg-Cuula. His ardent fighting spirit, unconditional belief in Victory and his unique sense for service until the very end gives this obituary testimony to all that had the great luck to know him.*" One of the bunkers of the Company was named after him and a birch cross erected in his memory on the place where he died.

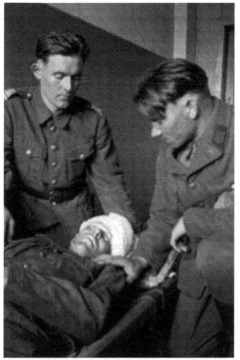

The body of Gösta Hallberg-Cuula with his comrades.

His body received a Christian ceremony at Sandudds Chapel at Helsinki the 30th April and moved to Stockholm to receive military honours.

The controversy

He was buried at the Norra Kirkogården in Stockholm the 9th May 1942, where his grave is still considered as an historical item protected by the Swedish Culture department[7]. On the stone the motto *Fjärran i Öster fallen för Sverige* (Far in East fallen for Sweden) can be read. The burial ceremony received great attention by the mass media, being represented by many high ranking military officers despite the fact that it was organized by the National Socialist party. The youth organization dedicated the cover of their monthly magazine *Ungt Folk* (Young People) to *"Sveriges tapparaste frontsoldat har gått til Valhall"* (Sweden's most courageous frontline soldier has departed for Valhalla) with the classic portrait of him wearing the party symbol on his right breast on the uniform as well as the clasp with all his decorations[8]. The 14th April was proclaimed by the party leader, Lindholm, as *Den Stupades Dag* (The Fallen's Day) to be commemorated each year, a tradition that was kept even when the party was dissolved 1950 by veterans and nowadays by Swedish nationalist groups. The Frontfighter's section of the party renamed their unit at the Finnish Front to *Kampavdelning Hallberg-Cuula* on his honnour, as the members in the Waffen-SS did it to *Hans Lindén* (one of the first party members KIA, who enlisted at 17 years of age, deceased December 1941 serving in the *Wiking* division).

Party pin of the Sveaborg branch.

Hallberg-Cuula's graveyard in Stockholm.

The leftist parties and mass media tried to dishonour him by arguing that he was Finnish and not really a Swedish national. Even today many publications still spread these rumors.

Propaganda poster edited by the SSS party. *"Many gave their lives for Sweden's freedom and the Nordic culture. What are you sacrifying?"*.

Cover of the magazine of the Youth Organization of the party remembrance of the Hero.

His mother reacted immediately and made it known widely that he was in fact the son of a Swedish citizen and that she was from a Swedish family, that Gösta Hallberg-Cuula never considered himself as a Finn despite the fact that he admired and loved this country so much that he gave his life for its freedom[9]. His military file at the Finnish War Archive clearly reflects that he was a Swedish volunteer and that his mother tongue was Swedish with a knowledge of the Finnish language that was almost none ("some") but that he spoke English and German fluently. When he was killed in action, the Finnish HQ published, as usual, his necrology in the Finnish press remarking also that he was a foreign volunteer.

Note

[1] War Archive, Helsinki, Military file Gösta Hallberg-Cuula.

[2] DSN, issues numbers 32/1933; 50/1934; 100/1935; 99/1936.

[3] *SE*, bildtidning, Stockholm, nr.26/30.III.1940.

[4] A complete reportage at the Finnish-Swedish newspaper *Västra Nyland*, 17.VII.1941, *"Hos Hallberg-Cuulas djärva främlingspluton I Hangöeld"* (With Hallberg-Cuula's brave Foreing platoon below fire at Hangö). In this Finnish newspaper he is presented as a Swedish Officer, not as Finnish.

[5] DSF (Den Svenske Folksocialisten), 25.IV.1942, p.8, *"Hallberg-Cuula talar"* (Hallberg-Cuula talks).

[6] Despite in Swedish, the most accurate history of this unit is *Svenskarna vid Jandeba. Svenska Frivilligkompaniet 1942-1944*, by von SCHMIDT-LAUSSITZ, Luleå, Förlag Svenskafrivilliga, 2007.

[7] http://norrabegravningsplatsen.se/sten-nr-523-gosta-hallberg-cuula.

[8] UF, nr. 4/1942.

[9] DSF, 19.XII.1942, "Hallberg-Cuula var helt igenom svensk" (Hallberg-Cuula was completely Swedish), signed by Otto Hallberg and Fanny Hallberg-Cuula.

WW2 AXIS
FORCES

Made in the USA
Middletown, DE
17 February 2020